Pluralism: Cultural M

Multilingual Matters

MULTILINGUAL MATTERS 11

Pluralism: Cultural Maintenance and Evolution

Brian M. Bullivant
Reader in Education
Monash University

MULTILINGUAL
MATTERS LTD

British Library Cataloguing in Publication Data

Bullivant, Brian M
    Pluralism. — (Multilingual matters; 11)
    1. Pluralism (Social sciences) — Australia
    2. Australia — Ethnic relations
    I. Title   II. Series
    305   DU120

    ISBN 0-905028-27-9
    ISBN 0-905028-26-0 Pbk

Multilingual Matters Ltd,
Bank House, 8a Hill Road,
Clevedon, Avon BS21 7HH,
England.

Typeset by Wayside Graphics, Clevedon, Avon.
Printed and bound in Great Britain by
Short Run Press Ltd, Exeter EX2 7LW.

To Jenny

Contents

Foreword

Cultural pluralism or multiculturalism has become a feature of many Western countries during this century in at least two ways. Firstly, cultural pluralism in the sense of cultural diversity is an obvious fact. Countries such as the United States, Canada, Britain, Australia and New Zealand contain significant numbers of racial and ethnic groups and segments which preserve parts of their cultures, and follow life-styles that differ in many ways from those of the majority population. Secondly, cultural pluralism or multiculturalism has been adopted at the official levels of government and semi-government as a socio-political philosophy to help guide policy-making in such vital areas as education, social welfare and even law.

But, whether as fact or philosophy, the concept of cultural pluralism can also obscure more than it illuminates. Factually, cultural pluralism or diversity is almost invariably thought of as applying only to differences in lifestyles. These are essentially private concerns and, with only few exceptions, do not flow over into the public domain of society and affairs of the state. Yet it is here that one's life chances are determined in the sense of gaining equality of access to a share of socio-economic rewards and resources. Claims by government and semi-government officials that cultural pluralism (or other pluralist policies) will enhance equality of opportunity can conceal the real issue, which is bound up with the way power is controlled and allocated in a modern nation–state. It is possible to demonstrate this convincingly by tracing how ideologies of pluralism evolve historically in response to economic and political changes in the social system. Australia is used as an example in Chapters 2 and 3 to demonstrate this inescapable feature of pluralism, which can be found in all Western societies.

Can the maintenance of cultural pluralism or multiculturalism have a positive value for ethnocultural groups? Philosophically it is tempting to point to the ways in which a society is enriched by the cultural diversity brought into it by its constituent ethnocultural groups, and it would be naïve to ignore these advantages. A more important consideration, however, is whether the maintenance of cultural diversity can have positive *survival value* for the groups concerned. Must they always and inevitably assimilate into the dominant society and its culture, or are there ways by which cultural programmes can be preserved or modified to suit modern conditions?

Australian Aborigines, discussed in Chapters 1 and 4, may seem an unusual choice as an example to illustrate how cultural programmes can be adapted to assist an ethnocultural group to survive under conditions that are very different from those that existed when the programmes first evolved. But what is more at issue here is the *principle of structural and cultural adaptation* that applies to any ethnocultural group, and not the specific details of any one cultural programme. Australian Aborigines illustrate in a most striking way how a culture of great antiquity was first developed under very specific conditions of desert and coastal fringe survival, yet despite this uniqueness can still be adapted to cope with the impact of the West, even in a modern urban setting.

More important, however, is the light this Aboriginal example throws on a closely-related principle that is at the heart of survival. This is the need for cultural pluralism to be complemented by structural or institutional pluralism if an ethnocultural group is to have any real chance of resisting assimilation and gaining advantages in terms of access to socio-economic rewards and resources. Aboriginal groups in Australian society owe much of their successes since 1970 to the fact that they have been able to politicize their claims on the wider society, and force the setting up of institutions that serve their needs in education, housing, social welfare and health. The solutions adopted and discussed in Chapter 4 range from separatism to a form of assimilation, but in each of them the message for other ethnocultural groups is clear: survival depends as much on an economic, structural base as on the ideational base that is culture. In short, cultural pluralism without the corollary of structural pluralism dooms an ethnic group to inevitable assimilation in the long run. In Chapters 2 and 3 these principles are also examined in relation to Australian race relations, immigration and position of migrants. The evolution of ideologies of pluralism such as assimilation and multiculturalism is discussed. Anglo-Celtic dominance or hegemony is shown to operate through education despite official claims to the contrary.

This book then is about a number of *principles* of cultural pluralism or multiculturalism and the survival of racial and ethnic groups in pluralist society. Such principles tend to be overlooked if one concentrates only on the welter of information about the social, cultural and other pluralist characteristics of any society, yet understanding the underlying principles that motivate relations between its racial and ethnic groups may point a way towards solutions for the problems pluralism poses.

I am most grateful to the Faculty of Education, Monash University, for a grant of leave to undertake an outside studies programme of further research in this area. My special thanks are due to Professor Kenneth Kirkwood, Rhodes Professor of Race Relations at Oxford University, for his kind invitation to work on these issues at St Antony's College during the whole of Trinity Term, 1983. He encouraged me to revise and augment a series of seminar papers I gave there into a form suitable for wider publication. As on previous occasions I benefited greatly from discussions with Professor Michael Banton at the University of Bristol, whose incisive comments have prompted clarification of my own ideas.

However, whatever limitations they still contain are due as much to the restrictions on space and compression of supporting data that are inherent in a seminar format, as to the stage of development that my thinking has now reached since an earlier work, *The Pluralist Dilemma in Education: Six Case Studies*. That I have been able to partially overcome the former, by revising the seminar papers for this book, and persevere with the latter, owes a great deal to the encouragement and forbearance of my wife Jenny, to whom the final product is dedicated.

Brian M. Bullivant

Monash University
November 1983

1 Maintenance of traditional culture

The mystique of land in Aboriginal tradition

Central to any consideration of cultural pluralism must be the concept of culture. Unless precision is achieved about what it means, discussion and thinking about the relationships this kind of pluralism may involve can easily degenerate into trite statements and superficial claims. It is also necessary to understand the concept in order to recognize some of the reasons why social, political and economic relations between dominant and subordinate ethnocultural groups within pluralist societies almost inevitably involve competition and often outright conflict, unless a policy of assimilating the minorities is adhered to and achieved.

The main driving force that leads to this result is the almost invariable compulsion individuals and groups have to maximize their perceived advantage *vis-à-vis* other individuals and groups. I have developed this argument more fully elsewhere (Bullivant, 1981b) and most recently it has been expressed by Professor Michael Banton (1983: 136 *et passim*) in terms of rational choice theory:

> ". . . according to which group members exchange goods and services, seeking their own advantage. If they compete with one another on an individual basis this will tend to dissolve group boundaries. If they compete as groups, their shared interests will lead them to reinforce those boundaries; the whole life and culture of the privileged group will be oriented to defending their exclusive boundary, while the life of the subordinated group will be directed towards the cultivation of their inclusive bonds so as to

1

mobilize strength for the attack upon the practices which
exclude them from privilege."

Culture, then, embodies strategies by which social groups maximize their perceived advantage relative to other groups. But it is more
than this. Culture is also a programme or blueprint to enable a society
to survive in its environment in such a way as to maximize what its
members take to be their best advantage. In addition, part of the
programme contains a set of ideas and beliefs — termed ideologies in
Chapter 2 — that justify or legitimate both the necessity for controlling
the environment in one way and not another, and for competing with
or even exterminating other groups that may be trying to maximize
their advantage. Culture thus contains not only survival instructions
but also often an elaborate justification for their type and purpose. The
chapter that follows develops these ideas.

Culture as a programme for survival

Thinking in cultural anthropology has come a long way since
Tylor (1871) defined culture as that "complex whole which includes
knowledge, belief, art, morals, law, customs, and any other capabil-
ities and habits acquired by man as a member of Society". Such an
enumeratively descriptive definition quickly leads to a conceptual
quagmire, as Schneider & Bonjean (1973: 120ff.) point out, as virtually everything gets to be included in the list of cultural traits,
eventually leading to definitional impotency. Indeed, culture may be
an "essentially contested concept", a term used by Gallie (1955–6) to
describe concepts that "inevitably involve endless disputes about their
uses on the part of their users". In an attempt to restore some order in a
rapidly burgeoning field, Kroeber & Kluckhohn (1952) produced a
definition which they evolved out of some two hundred definitions then
available in the literature. In their definition the importance of ideas and
their attached values as components of culture was emphasized.

Later developments in cognitive anthropology have stressed the
ideational aspect of culture. Thus Goodenough (1964: 36) maintains
that: "A society's culture consists of whatever it is one has to know or
believe in order to operate in a manner acceptable to its members." To
Keesing (1976) culture comprises ideational codes for living.

Marion Dobbert (1976: 207) takes an almost cybernetic view of culture, maintaining it "is a system for mapping information from an environment. This information is stored in shared conceptual patterns, in patterns for social interaction and in patterns for getting a living". Geertz (1966) also takes an ideational view of culture in considering the role of religion in social life. In a later work (Geertz, 1973) the importance of including behaviours in any consideration of culture is stressed, to obtain a "thick description". Redfield (1962: 238) took the same view: "A culture is an organization or integration of conventional understandings . . . [and] the acts and the objects . . . which express and maintain these understandings." A number of other theorists (e.g. Thompson, 1969; Cohen, 1971; Bock, 1969) go further in implying or explicitly stating what culture is for. In their view, it is a form of survival programme or device, whereby man in society copes with the environment in which he lives, and solves the problems it poses.

We can usefully extend these views, by going back to a number of basic ideas. People live in a society, and acquire its culture. They play a part in modifying and adapting it to meet current problems and future contingencies by rejecting irrelevant components no longer needed for survival, and introducing new ones. "Cultural lag" ensures that some aspects survive as traditions even when they may have no real relevance. Culture is thus not a static phenomenon, but is subject to regular evolution in response to the circumstances in which a society finds itself (Bidney, 1967: 27).

This is not a one-way, deterministic relationship, however, as a cultural programme is a response to what a society defines as its environment. To appreciate the force of this the environment can be thought of conceptually as three interdependent sub-environments. The first is the natural or geographical environment and habitat, together with their biotic and other resources. These can be valued in different ways by different societies. Thus, the granite outcrop that is so valuable to an Australian Aborigine, because it is an ancestral sacred site, may have no value for a European prospector. Conversely, an area containing oil-bearing strata may have no value for an Aborigine if it does not contain a sacred site, but would be of considerable importance to a European oil-driller. Values such as these are not fixed in time but change historically. Oil-bearing shales in Queensland were long known to exist but were not valued. It took the modern oil crisis to "attach" value to them. We can thus say with some justification that the value of the environment is not intrinsic to it, but is in the minds of those who inhabit the land.

The second conceptual sub-environment is a social one, consisting of those groups with which a society comes into contact. The third sub-environment is more speculative, but is required in order to account for the often elaborate systems of religious belief which relate man to an unseen world and its various "inhabitants". We can tentatively term this the metaphysical environment. It embodies a society's definitions of what is "out there" in terms of supernatural beings, forces and powers. An important part of many cultural programmes is the body of beliefs, creeds, rituals and ceremony that attempt to bring man into contact with this world. What should not be lost sight of, however, as Berger & Luckmann point out (1971), is that it constitutes a "symbolic universe" of man's own making. Despite the fact that the devout believer treats it as "real", nonetheless such "facticity" is a deception. The symbolic universe is a social construction, which is constantly being reified by those who have forgotten or choose to ignore its societal origins.

Building on the above conceptual foundations we define culture as an interdependent and patterned system of valued traditional and current public knowledge and conceptions, embodied in behaviours and artefacts, and transmitted to present and new members, both symbolically and non-symbolically, which a society has evolved historically and progressively modifies and augments, to give meaning to and cope with its definitions of present and future existential problems. It should be noted, if only in passing, that the most important method of communication is spoken and written language, strictly a system of signs rather than symbols — hence the use of the term "non-symbolically" in the above definition. In Leach's (1976) view, language is used symbolically when it has to refer to phenomena, such as those in a symbolic universe, that occupy a context not related to that of the sign itself. For example, the term "cross", meaning two intersecting lines at right angles, remains a sign in its mathematical context, but becomes symbolic when used to refer to the cross of the Christian faith and, by extension, metaphorically its belief system and practice, the "Way of the Cross".

The past and present orientation of a cultural survival programme is of significance when one considers a group such as Australian Aborigines. One might ask, for instance, to what extent are beliefs and knowledge derived from the ancient past still functionally relevant in helping them survive and cope with life in a modern, European industrial society. To what extent have Aborigines been able to adapt their culture to suit such an environment? Questions such as these have particular force when considered in relation to Aboriginal systems of land tenure, firstly as they existed in traditional times, secondly as they have been adapted to the twentieth century.

Religion and land in Aboriginal culture

Consideration of Aboriginal culture as it existed in traditional, pre-contact times can only be attempted in broad terms. For more detail the classical accounts by Elkin (1964) and Berndt & Berndt (1964) are available. Likewise, because of their great subtlety, it is impossible to do full justice to Aboriginal relationships to the land. As Professor Stanner pointed out in the 1968 Boyer Lectures, "no English words are good enough to give an adequate sense of the links between an Aboriginal group and its homeland". Some indication of the reason for this difficulty can be appreciated from the many meanings the Aboriginal word for *home* can have: "camp", "hearth", "country", "everlasting home", "totem place", "life source", "spirit centre", and, as Stanner remarks, "much else all in one" (Stanner, 1969: 44). While land has always been the economic base for Aborigines, it has also held considerable religious significance for them. In effect, it is difficult if not impossible, in the case of Aboriginal culture, to make the conceptual distinction between the metaphysical, social and natural environments that we set out above, so intimately did the Aborigine have a spiritual and personal relationship with the land. This fact and the central place religious beliefs occupy in Aboriginal life must be appreciated for understanding the reactions of Aborigines to the impact of Europeans and their culture.

In traditional times, some 250,000 Aborigines throughout Australia were semi-nomadic, travelling around in hunting-foraging, kinship groups or bands for which the term tribe is an inadequate and possibly misleading expression. Most certainly there were no chiefs leading the groups, nor the kinds of political structures familiar to students of African societies and cultures. The quasi-tribes usually numbered between 100 and 1,500 people, with population density varying from as high as one person to the square mile, in the case of the coastal groups where food and resources were abundant, to one person per 35 or more square miles in desert areas (Stevens, 1970: 364). Each quasi-tribe spoke a distinct language, and occupied a continuous tract of land. Again, "occupy" is a misleading word as it has European connotations of economic possession, when in fact the relationship was a much more symbiotic one. As Mr Justice Blackburn was to say of it in 1971, during the celebrated Yirrkala land rights case (Blackburn, 1971: 270–271) "it seems easier, on the evidence, to say that the clan belongs to the land than that the land belongs to the clan". As Stevens (ibid., p. 364) points out, however: "In some of the more well-watered areas there was a definite association between family groups and their rights to occupation of and produce from distinct geographical areas". Obtaining the produce was carried out through sexual division of labour. Men hunted and provided meat, especially from larger animals such as kangaroos. Women foraged, mainly for plants, roots and seeds, but also caught small animals and reptiles such as lizards or snakes. On the whole, women were more reliable food providers than men. In coastal areas fishing was as productive as hunting; this was also the case for tribes who lived along the Murray River. Use of the land rarely meant that all of an occupied piece of territory would be foraged or hunted over. Often the unproductive parts would not be visited except at times when rare seasonal rains brought a quick growth of plants or attracted game to temporary waterholes.

The sexual division of labour went far beyond merely utilizing the natural environment and its resources, but was an essential prerequisite for enabling the group's relationships with the metaphysical environment to function. Fostering these through the performance of various rituals and ceremonies was the responsibility of the men although women, too, had their own ceremonies. The sexual division of labour enabled men to devote time to art, ritual and other tribal matters. This would not have been possible had men been responsible for all the activities carried out by women, though Maddock's (1974: 25) view that these were menial and those of the men "aristocratic" is a distortion of what was a mutually supportive relationship. It was also essential, according to the Aboriginal world view, in that it allowed men to perform the religious rituals which would enhance the fertility of the land and increase the species of animals on which the Aborigines depended for survival. Where such specific "increase rites" were not performed, more generalized ceremonies were used to invoke beings or persons who were more widely associated with fertility in the Aboriginal cosmology, e.g. the "All-Mother, the Rainbow Serpent, and the *wondjina* spirits" (Maddock, 1974: 26).

To leave the description of man-land relationships there is to miss their subtlety, as it is necessary to consider the composition and arrangement of the social environment and group life in more detail, despite the notorious difficulty of doing so. However, this necessitates some prior consideration of the Aboriginal religion and metaphysical environment with which the whole of social relationships were involved. As Berndt & Phillips (1973: 31) have commented,

> "The truths of social living . . . were enshrined in their religion . . . A strong belief in that religion ensured maintenance of a social and cultural order that most of them [the Aborigines] seem to have regarded as eminently satisfactory. Within it they found recognition of the dignity of man as a person, an assurance that his life had pattern and meaning, and that in death he was not lost to his society: that an essential essence remained, and could never be dissipated."

Traditional Aboriginal religion is very ancient. As long ago as 30,000 BC Aborigines used art and ritual as part of their burial practices, as shown by excavations at Lake Mungo in New South Wales.

The concept of the Dreamtime holds a central place in traditional Aboriginal religion. It refers to the beginning or time of creation when the spirit ancestors emerged from their ancient resting places in an earth without form, or from the water. The spirit ancestors were the origin of all life and form, and were able to assume both animal and human characteristics. They moved over the land, fought, copulated, and took part in other activities which became the subject of detailed Aboriginal myths and legends. The activities and movements of the spirit ancestors produced shapes and features such as outcrops of rock, waterholes, rivers, caves, and other natural landmarks. Far from being just geomorphological or geological features, such landmarks became imbued with permanent, everlasting value as legendary mythical reminders of the creative spirit ancestors. Although they returned to their spirit homes — usually at distinctive and very sacred sites in the land — the spirit ancestors' spiritual essence, as it were, was left in the landmarks, the legendary tracks they followed during their wanderings, and the special sites commemorating their heroic deeds. Even after returning to their spirit homes, the spirit ancestors were still held in Aboriginal consciousness, for they were considered to maintain a watchful presence over what they had created and to be perenially responsive to the need for continuing the creation through involvement in the cycle of birth, life, death.

Conception was thus thought of in human and religious terms. The Dreamtime ancestors were the source of each person's spirit, which was sent into the womb of a woman at conception to join with the corporeal body made by the mother following impregnation. Body and introduced spirit united to form the child, with the father's role being to ritually discern and direct the activity of the creative spirit. At birth, the child belonged to the same spirit group as the father, and shared not only the same ancestral spirit but also the natural species symbol or totem linked to it.

Here we have another overlap between all three sub-environments conceptualized above. In the Aboriginal belief system animals and birds and reptiles were held to be living symbols or totems of the spirit ancestors and certain tracts of land. Particular totemic animals, say, the crow or goanna, would be associated with the father's country. All those from the same country by birth belonged to a totemic clan or religious group. Usually, but not invariably, one's membership in this was determined by descent from the father, i.e. paternal filiation. An alternative term for totem in Aboriginal mythology is one's "dreaming", shared by all those belonging to the same natural species or totem clan. The dreaming was a permanent reminder to all members of a particular clan that they shared the same spirit ancestor and were thus related. As a sign of respect for the spirit ancestor's totem and to indicate that it shared a common origin and life with the clan members, they would not hurt the symbolic natural species or totem, and commonly would refrain from eating it. Thus members of a clan whose totem was the ring-tailed possum, would not include this animal in their diet. Going further, because members of a clan were spiritually related to one another marriage between each other was regarded as incestuous and forbidden. Thus patrilineal totem clans were exogamous, and complex rules were established to prevent inter-marriage. As a result of paternal filiation combined with exogamy, a child could not belong to his or her mother's clan, but could nevertheless enjoy some rights to its land (Maddock, 1974: 30).

This discussion does not exhaust the topic of clan membership by any means. There were, for example, maternally filiated clans where the child, male or female, was assigned to the mother's clan, and conception clans, formed by conception filiation. The underlying principle of this type was that the clan consisted "of all those persons whose mothers were spiritually fecundated by contact with a power of the same species, for example, euro, honey ant, native cat. Clans of this type are not exogamous . . ." (ibid., p. 31).

Clans owned or shared tracts of land in the sense of having a "religiously sanctioned *estate* in land", and being linked to the spirit ancestor through totemic association. However, a distinction can be made between this arrangement and the band, "an aggregate of persons making use of a *range* of land" (ibid., p. 32). In short, "A clan . . . has title to land; a band, licence to use land". Aborigines from one clan might wander into another clan's land in the course of hunting or foraging but would not share its deep sense of spiritual origins. These would exert a pull which would always be attracting Aborigines back to their own land, in the sense of estate.

Such links were not solely of ancient historical importance. The power of the Dreamtime and an individual or clan's particular dreaming continues in perpetuity. As Maddock has noted (ibid., p. 27):

> "The tie between men and land is taken back to The
> Dreaming. Human rights to land are as old as the present
> shape of the earth and spring from the very personnages
> who gave the earth its shape . . . The Aboriginal theory is
> thus that rights to land have to do with the design of the
> world, not with alienable land title."

Much of Aboriginal regard for land today stems from this base and is
historically and spiritually continuous with the Dreamtime. It is essential to appreciate this fundamental fact for a full understanding of the
contemporary fight for social justice and land rights.

The Dreamtime and the temporal world

Leaving description at that point would be to overlook other
subtle relationships in the Aboriginal world view, the damage to which
has been further reasons for the decline of the Aborigines' morale. The
Dreamtime and religious beliefs also influenced social relationships
and other aspects of the temporal world. The spirit ancestors and their
activities and social relationships were not merely part of an elaborate
cosmological construction but were prototypes for Aboriginal social
life. Rules regarding this, and all aspects of daily living, were embodied in what was termed The Law. Access to The Law was peren-
nially available to the Aborigine through meditation, prayer and the
performance of rituals, usually though not invariably·at the sacred sites
associated with the totemic spirit ancestors. Ritual enabled Aborigines
to get in touch with their dreaming at any time, and this provided
pattern and predictability to daily living as recourse to the guiding
principles of life could always be obtained. As Berndt & Phillips (1973:
31) have explained (a lengthy quotation is justified):

> "The Dreaming, then, permeated all aspects of living. It
> was certainly not a mystical concept. It was neither wholly
> spiritual, nor wholly material. Rather, it imbued the mun-
> dane, the ordinary things of living and thinking (natural-
> physical and psycho-social) with a spiritual character and
> intimacy. The Aborigines were utterly dependent on their
> environment. Mostly, though not necessarily in bad seasons,

they were secure in the certainty that they had behind them (in many cases within them) the great mythic beings. Without them, the Aborigines would have been lost. It was, however, not just a matter of these beings existing. Their interest had to be sustained. Human beings had to do their part, as the spirit beings had already done theirs. The visible evidence of their contribution was in the environment itself. Man had to make sure that continuity was maintained. And this is what ritual was really about. Aboriginal man performed religious rituals for this purpose, among other and more secondary reasons . . .

One of the really remarkable features of Aboriginal life is the time devoted to ritual matters, to music, song, dance, and to the making of emblems and objects, and to the telling of myths. In all areas of Australia, in the face of an ever-present need to search for food, the Aborigines found time for these activities — not just a little time, but an abundant amount of it. They were attuned so well to their environment and to the routine of living that this was possible in the more arid as well as in the fertile regions of this continent. This was partly because religion was seen as *an essential element in the pattern of work*, as having a crucial, utilitarian bearing on social living. Involvement in ritual affairs was not viewed as a leisure-time activity, but as a necessity in the sequence of economic survival."

It would not be going too far to say that, for an Aborigine, deprivation of the opportunity, time and land-sacred site association for the performance of rituals would cut him off from spiritual and economic reasons for wanting to survive.

The need to perform rituals and the responsibility this task entailed have already been noted in relation to male-female, sexual division of labour. It also played a major part in determining seniority and ranking in Aboriginal bands. All in an Aboriginal community shared in the expression and celebration of their religion to a lesser or greater degree through the religious rituals, dancing, arts, singing and telling myths. However, just how much participation was permissible rested on the rules regarding the degree of access to valued religious knowledge allowed to each member of the community. In broad terms differentiation was made on an age/experience grading and a sexual basis. Uninitiated men/boys or women/girls had much less access than initiated men. Their access increased with age and passage through other initiation ceremonies into more esoteric bodies of knowledge. This should not be confused with the age-grade initiation system practised in parts of Africa.

The major responsibility for safeguarding, practising and trans- mitting the religious rituals and their validating bodies of knowledge rested with the initiated men. As a man acquired more knowledge, his personal power and respect increased commensurately, so that full knowledge and considerable power often came to repose in the per- sons of old men. They were the ultimate custodians of religious know- ledge, its rights and responsibilities, the spiritual caretakers and heirs to their clan's estate, and keepers of all the sacred objects associated with the ritual-spirit ancestor-land-Dreamtime synthesis. The sacred objects held great religious significance and were guarded vigilantly, especially from the eyes of women and the uninitiated who could ritually contaminate them and reduce their power. This was essential, as the sacred objects — commonly carved or painted boards and stones — were the ritual means by which the spirit ancestors could be invoked and made to be immanent in the Aborigines' thinking. Without such rituals and their objects (called *tjuringa* in Central Australia and *rangga* in Northern Australia) the link with the Dreamtime and the present could not be established, thus its power and guiding principles could not be brought to bear on contemporary survival problems, ensuring the continuity of natural species, the fertility of the land, and the well-being of the band.

To some extent, Aboriginal society was ruled by a gerontocracy but only in religious and ritual matters, though the seniority and power associated with them spilled over into more mundane matters such as political relationships between tribes or social relationships within a band. Most definitely there was no form of cultic priesthood in the sense of an intermediary between man and the divinity. As Maddock (1974: 43) explains:

"There was no suggestion of a professional, still less an hereditary, priesthood separated from the rest of the population. Every man's religious standing increased with age as he deepened his experience and expertise in his society's lore and ritual, provided only that he remained active and in possession of his faculties. His special rights in one situation, for example managerial authority or privileged access to restricted places, gave him no overall advantage, because all his fellows enjoyed equivalent rights in other situations."

The interlocking nature of Aboriginal religion was (and partly still is) at the basis of the lack of a cultic priesthood. No one clan was the holder of all the traditions and beliefs associated with any one spirit ancestor let alone all spirit ancestors. Each clan had a share of the total religious heritage and at ceremonial occasions made its contribution to activities that was distinctive. Joint ceremonies involving several clans were quite common, though considerable variation existed in their frequency and ritual content throughout Australia. Mutual dependence and, probably more importantly, denying clans autonomy in the performance of their rituals (Maddock, 1974: 37), were at the heart of Aboriginal religion, and its organization or working arrangements. Of more significance today is that inability to perform rituals due to European interference, such as seizure of land, has effects that are not confined to one locality, but have ramifications, wherever there are clans, which collaborate in the collective ceremonies of which the interrupted rituals form a part.

Social and kinship groupings

Mutual dependence and inter-clan links were also provided for through the kinship and marriage system of Aborigines — probably one of the strongest aspects of their culture to survive into the present. Because of their great complexity only the broad aspects can be touched on.

Aborigines belonged to a social or kinship group in addition to their religious clan affiliation. Membership of a kinship group was also determined by birth and was matrilineal in most cases. Its function was to regulate marriage and human relationships, which it bound together with strong ties that played a part in maintaining Aboriginal senses of identity as a people and Aboriginal brotherhood.

Unlike one's membership of a religious clan, membership in a kinship equivalent does not depend on the possession of religious knowledge or ritual responsibilities. Instead, the kinship membership was based on the "skin" or "flesh" relationships of an individual. Marriage outside one's social or "flesh" group was the rule, linked to complicated patterns of group divisions and classifications. "Kinship and society are coextensive; that is, all persons with whom an Aborigine deals socially are classed as kin of his . . . The relation in which two persons stand to each other regulates their behaviour; that is, a kinship system defines behaviour as well as classifying persons" (Maddock, 1974: 45–46).

However, classes and kinship groups also have a wider religious function in two senses. "Skin" or "flesh" groups have their religiously-based symbols or totems. Thus divisions associated with different totems, such as the moiety ("half") type, are related to different roles and responsibilities, privileges and duties in religious celebrations, initiation rites or funerary ceremonies. An Aborigine is thus at the focus of a number of interlocking networks and their associated totem symbols (Maddock, 1974: 88):

> "The value of classes in facilitating the working out of relations is seen also in the use made of them to determine responsibilities in the religious cults, the performance of which provides an occasion for scores or hundreds of people, some of whom would otherwise seldom meet, to gather together. Class systems lend themselves to the expansion of sociability and, like the kin systems with which they are correlated and the religious cults upon which they so often impress their pattern, must be regarded as among the universalistic features of Aboriginal culture."

The strength of the religion-nature-society relationships is very strong. In effect, a person is at the focal point of the three interlocking systems or sub-environments, as we have termed them. Maintaining harmony in one has inevitable effects on the others. The Law sets out rules for all three. One can now appreciate that enforced rule-breaking due to the exigencies created by European contact has far-reaching effects that Europeans cannot fully comprehend, as their world view is based on a separation of the three systems. What can be at stake for Aborigines if a rule is broken in one of them is the survival of the other two (Maddock, 1974: 89, 108):

> "When nature is shaped after the social order, he who breaks a rule is in breach of natural as well as social law. He disturbs the integration of social relationships with relationships between society and the surrounding cosmos . . . Given the unity of society and nature that Aborigines assert in their cosmology, it is not to be wondered at that the impending ruin of their social order should be prefigured in the fear that the cosmic order was about to collapse upon them."

Two contrasting world views towards land

The impending ruin of the Aboriginal social order started in 1788 when the First Fleet set up settlement in New South Wales. To fully comprehend the magnitude of what would befall the Aborigines, whose whole existence — temporal and spiritual — was invested in the land, it is instructive to attempt a summary of how this vital component was regarded at the time by Europeans and Aborigines. The summary draws heavily and almost exclusively on Yarwood & Knowling (1982: 11ff.).

(i) The British view

Land was an economic resource and the basis of considerable social status and power in Britain. Although it also had some sentimental importance, land could be sold and title to the estate transferred to new owners, because it was a possession like any other good. The

British were thus able to move away from a piece of land they sold without a great emotional wrench if it was advantageous to do so. While occupying land, they were able to farm it and hunt on it without seeing how these two activities might be incompatible.

Possessions and material goods, of which land formed a part, were at the heart of British culture. Early settlers thus followed a similar pattern of establishing private ownership of land in a tangible way by fencing or tilling it, grazing herds of cattle or flocks of sheep on it, building houses and making equipment to further utilize the land. In this they were exploitative, having little regard for the delicate ecological balance in which the land had existed for centuries. They legitimated this activity by their religious, Christian ideology which can be summed up by the term "Protestant ethic".

The early settlers saw that the Aborigines had made no impact on the land and thus regarded them as having no claim to it, as it was not being used. They legitimated their seizure of title to the land — a concept alien to Aboriginal thinking — by myths about Aborigines' dirtiness, licentiousness and barbarity. These were used to justify a policy of exterminating Aborigines — a fate they richly deserved as a species much lower in the evolutionary order than the high-status, white races.

(ii) The Aboriginal view

The spiritual importance of the land was as compelling as, or even transcended, the economic importance of the land. Its physical features were often of totemic significance, thus embracing both social and cosmological realms. Land could neither be owned, held in title, nor sold or transferred; such concepts being alien to Aboriginal thinking. One could not be separated from nor leave one's land without being emotionally affected to the very core of one's being. Separation from places meant separation from everything that held the key to Aboriginal understanding of life and regeneration of the world, its natural and social resources. Separation from their land for Aborigines meant losing a vital part of their reason for existence in spiritual terms, if not also in purely physical or temporal terms.

From such a view, the British violated sacred sites and desecrated the land by the exploitative use they made of it. Thus the co-existence of farming and hunting techniques were not possible and could not be condoned. They offended the static conservative approach to land that was basic to Aboriginal thinking, and attempted to preserve resources from excessive exploitation, so maintaining the delicate balance of natural species essential to economic survival and the totemic order of religious life.

Aboriginal culture and the twentieth century

Following First Settlement, Aboriginal numbers were decimated from an estimated total of 250,000 in 1788 to a low point of 66,099 in 1933.[1] British brutality and policies of extermination, introduced diseases against which Aborigines had no resistance, malnutrition, and shattered morale and will to live, were all factors contributing to the decimation. Numbers started to increase so that by the 1976 Census the total stood at 160,915 persons (Yarwood & Knowling, 1982: 258–9). Accompanying this change in numbers has been a change in the distribution of Aborigines following an extensive movement to the big cities since 1960. About 80,000 people of Aboriginal descent are urban dwellers, about 25,000 live on or about church missions or in their own settlements in the outback mainly in the Northern Territory. The remaining Aborigines live on pastoral properties or on the fringes of country towns (Engel, 1978; Australian Information Service, 1976).

To what exent do these changes mean changes in the traditional culture? In central, Northern and Northwestern Australia Aborigines still live in close contact with their traditional tribal beliefs though they are no longer hunting and foraging nomads. There is a duality in their belief systems, as many, who have ostensibly converted to Christianity on a mission or settlement, have still maintained their traditional beliefs. As might be expected, this is not so markedly the case with Aborigines in the country towns and cities where there is much less contact with the formalities and rituals of the traditional religious beliefs. However, this does not mean that Aborigines are any less spiritual or religious, merely that their culture may be re-establishing in a changed way, utilizing different forms of expression and basic, motivating force, as discussed in Chapter 4.

The Noonkanbah issue which erupted fully in August 1980, but had its origins a year before, is an example of the way Aborigines' close contact with their traditional beliefs came into conflict with a Western, oil-mining company's economic exploitation. Noonkanbah is a 400,000 hectare cattle station near Fitzroy Crossing, some 1,800 kilometres north of Perth. The station is leased from the Western Australian State Government under a scheme set up by the Federal Government in 1976 to enable purchase of land through the Aboriginal Land Fund.[2] The station is run and managed by a self-governing Aboriginal community, of a few hundred men, women and children, and with the name of Yungngora which means "The land is everything to us". The community has even set up and runs its own privately-financed bilingual school, where the children are taught to read and write English as well as cherish their own culture (Aboriginal Research Centre, 1982).

Memories of the past experiences of Aborigines throughout the north west of Western Australia are kept alive in stories told to children, such as the account of the 1926 Oombulgurri massacre. In this, Aborigines were driven in chains through the bush to be systematically slaughtered by a party of police and white pastoralists, as retribution for the spearing of one white man by an Aborigine, who thought his land was being invaded. It took 42 pack horses to carry supplies for the posse and these included 500 rounds of ammunition. A subsequent Royal Commission was only able to establish the deaths of a dozen or so Aborigines, although local tradition insists that many more were killed. No one was punished, not even the white participant in the massacre who advertised his plan to kill as many Aborigines as he could in an advance letter to a Perth newspaper, as the Royal Commissioner noted at the time of the Commission's enquiry.

Noonkanbah had been no stranger to white interference even prior to the oil mining issue. In 1978 it had been the venue for a giant corroboree of 15,000 men and women from all over the north who had gathered in direct response to a new kind of white pressure to form the

Kimberley Land Council. That pressure had been caused by diamond hunters swarming over the area and the Noonkanbah property pegging out about 200 leases, breaking down fences and terrifying cattle by prospecting from helicopters. The Aborigines appealed in the law courts against the mining but a mining warden's court ruled against them — the rights to prospect for minerals anywhere in Australia being almost inviolable.

In June 1979, the Noonkanbah people used legal tactics and threats of spearing prospectors from the giant American mineral exploration company Amax to drive off attempts to drill for oil on one of their sacred sites. Amax had a permit which had been granted by the State Government against the advice of one of its own anthropologists. The people of Noonkanbah also sent a spokesman on the long journey to Perth to appeal for public support for their cause. In an interview with reporters of *The Age*, a Melbourne-based newspaper, on 6 September 1979 he stated that Amax wanted to bulldoze sacred sites to get samples of rock. "If they destroy our lands this way our spirits will die. I go to the Christian church but I believe in Aboriginal law too. Our spirits will all die if they disturb our land." Despite this plea Amax went ahead with preparations to move one of its oil-drilling rigs to the station, and the convoy finally got under way by the 8th of August in the following year, 1980.

Meanwhile the ideological war had hotted up, with the Western Australian Government using every legal and, at times, quite racist tactic to discredit the Aboriginal case. A strong police cordon was put around the oil rig when it was dismantled at a site just to the north of Perth, and police cars and motor cycles guarded it as it began to move north to Noonkanbah. The Western Australian Government passed special legislation through State Parliament gazetting part of the Noonkanbah lease a public highway and the drilling site as a public open lease. Road rules and traffic regulations could therefore be applied, and police stopped every driver on, or entering the station to check driving licences. This was interpreted by Aborigines as a form of harassment.

By this time Noonkanbah had become a national issue involving the Federal Government, the Australian Council of Trade Unions, Anglican bishops, unionists and other pressure groups. The Western

Australian ruling Liberal government adopted an intransigent stand on the oil exploration issue, which no longer was the main motive behind its support for Amax. It was disclosed that the State Government could face a compensation claim of up to $2 million if Amax had been disallowed exploratory drilling on Noonkanbah because of reports by a State anthropologist. The issue also became an international one when the National Aboriginal Conference decided to send a delegation to Geneva to address a United Nations Human Rights Commission on the Noonkanbah question.[3] Aborigines also threatened to call on black Africans to support their cause by boycotting the Commonwealth Games in 1982 in Brisbane.

Aborigines' comments at the time reveal the depth of their feelings about the desecration to the sacred site on Noonkanbah, which had been fenced off by police and prospectors as part of the drilling area. The comments were collected by an Aborigine, Robert Bropho, on a journey through the outback Aboriginal settlements to canvass the opinions of Aboriginal elders or tribal lawmen. Some random selections: "If the Government and the mining corporations, if they're going to start moving and forcing their way into these sacred sites, it's going to go from one sacred site to another and there will be no place for them, for the Aboriginal people. We'll have no more place of worship and the tribal laws will fade away and they'll have nothing to step back on to" (Bill Wesley, tribal Aboriginal spokesman, Eastern Goldfields). "Government he taken this for nothing when black fella live there just like a kangaroo under a dry tree. But that land, he a human being, he belong to Australia. Now what more Government asking for? Put an oil rig there some place, sacred place, at Noonkanbah. Black fella got no hope at all. He only fallen people. That bloke, white fella, he taken country away from that black fella. White fella, he must give him back little plot." (Billy Gibbs, tribal old man of Jigalong). "We're crying here for our law" (Darson Wumi, tribal old man of Jigalong).[4]

It should be noted that the significance for Aborigines of the sacred site at Noonkanbah lay in the belief that under it lies the Great Goanna Spirit of the Dreamtime. It is the spiritual guardian of the local tribe, its land and everything born there. Without this protection the tribe cannot exist.

As is usual in Australia, the dispute dragged on for weeks, involved just about everybody with an axe to grind, a political gain to be made, or a grudge to repay, and ultimately fizzled out when it was disclosed that the Noonkanbah people were divided on the matter. Some wanted oil drilling to go ahead in the hope of obtaining royalties, others were adamantly opposed to it. In the event it did go ahead and the whole affair quickly became a dead issue, but not before it had shown how traditional beliefs of great antiquity could become embroiled in political, legal and economic considerations which involved national bodies and even got as far as an international forum.

Cultural adaptation and accommodation

Noonkanbah and other examples of Aboriginal settlements operating under various leasing arrangements, represent one attempt to come to terms with European influence. Others will be described in the fourth chapter of this book, to illustrate the several stages and strategies that Aborigines have adopted since the 1960s. Each appears to be an attempt at accommodation with some aspects of white culture and European economy while retaining as much of their traditional Aboriginal world view as possible. Inevitably these have had to be considerably modified in the process, but it would be erroneous to see this as merely one of assimilation or passive acquiescence to white man's culture. In Professor Stanner's (1979: 60–62) view:

> ". . . the Aborigines are widely in an obscure struggle with us . . . the essence of the struggle is their wish to go their own way . . . The one thing that seems to continue is the effort of the restless, if baffled, Aborigines to work out terms of life they know how to handle. That is why they develop rather than alter, substitute rather than forego, and give in only to try to outwit. Plainly visible through the process is the fact that it has a system, as every process must. It is as plain as daylight that this system is still fundamentally Aboriginal in type."

If only at the ideological level, i.e. that of ideas and beliefs, Aboriginal culture may be evolving as a counter to the pressures posed by Western, white dominance. However, in its turn, the ideological part of Western culture as held by the Anglo-Celtic dominant section of Australian society has also been evolving. This has partly been a corollary of changing technological, social, economic and other circumstances, and partly as a result of having to respond to pressures from outside Australia. Such a process began from the moment European settlers first came to Australia, and can be expected to continue, such is the evolutionary nature of culture and the drive to maximize group advantage that is at its foundation. It is a drive that has affected relationships with other minority groups besides Aborigines, and in the next chapter these are described in terms that attempt to illustrate how the drive to maximize advantage can be justified ideologically, no matter how bizarre and often nonsensical such legitimation may appear, from the standpoint of history and with the benefit of hindsight. There are many advantages in such an analysis, and conceivably it may even help to prevent similar mistakes being perpetrated in the present. "No one can throw off or succeed in ignoring the past, and only if its influence is examined can its power to mislead be corrected" (Banton, 1983: 14).

Notes to Chapter 1

1. The figure suggested by L.R. Smith (1980: 2–3, 10–55) based on a number of independent sources.
2. One of the structural institutions discussed more fully in Chapter 4 by which Aborigines have achieved greater control over their own life chances.
3. The National Aboriginal Conference is another new organization which, in this case, has enabled Aborigines to politicize and press their claims for justice.
4. These and other details of the dispute have been collected into a mimeographed booklet by the Aboriginal Research Centre, Monash University, Clayton, Victoria, Australia.

2 Challenge from hegemony and ideology

Race and ethnic relations in Australia from First Settlement to the 1960s

Nearly two hundred years have elapsed since Anglo-Celtic settlers became established in Australia and set in train the sequence of events that involved firstly relations between them and Aborigines, then Chinese, and finally other immigrants and settlers from a great variety of origins, who have flooded into the country especially in the post-Second World War years.[1] Each group has endeavoured to preserve or gain access to socio-economic rewards and resources and, by doing so, has come into competition and, at times, open conflict with other groups. Accompanying these relationships have been clear ideological claims which have attempted to justify one group's dominance over others. In any sense of the word, Australia since First Settlement has been a pluralist society — culturally, racially, socially, ethnically — and ideological claims have inevitably incorporated what have virtually been separate systems of ideas and beliefs about pluralist relations, i.e. ideologies of pluralism. In this chapter their influence on inter-group relations is conceptualized by means of a theoretical model, which is illustrated by taking a historical perspective on events and ideologies that have evolved since First Settlement until the 1960s.

The choice of the latter date is not entirely arbitrary. Until the end of the 1960s the evolution of the ideologies of pluralism propagated by the dominant Anglo-Celtic group can be traced with some certainty, although it is hardly an edifying story. The 1970s and subsequent years have seen so many changes in official policy and ideologies about immigrants that another chapter which follows this is needed to do them justice.

Maximizing advantage in race and ethnic relations

As they figure prominently in discussions about relations in pluralist societies, the terms "race" and "ethnic" must be clarified even though both are the subject of considerable argument and inaccurate usage. The term "race" is often used loosely and consequently erroneously to refer to groups of people regardless of whether they can be distinguished as having been descended from a common genetic stock. Thus, for example, one finds reference to the "Jewish race", but there are blond Jews, black Jews (Falashas from Ethiopia, for example), Yemeni Jews, white Jews, Moroccan Jews and many others. To say that they constitute one "race" is arrant nonsense, but one still finds this classificatory or typological approach used in some textbooks.

A more common usage of the concept of race is as a blanket term to refer to visible phenotypical differences between groups of people in skin colour, eye shape, hair texture and other physical characteristics. But strictly, these are all one sees. It is an inference from such evidence, and a culturally or often historically influenced inference at that, to claim that people possessing such-and-such characteristics belong to one "race". Scientifically, one's genetic origins can be established only by seriological (blood cell) analysis, but even this is questionable, and most certainly no basis for being able to establish a person's or group's "race" for the purpose of maintaining social relationships.

"Ethnic" ("ethnicity") is another concept, of more recent origin in the social science literature, about which opinions differ. It, too, has become a blanket term used to refer to virtually every distinguishing characteristic from social class or status to cultural traditions to "racial" features (see an excellent discussion in Lepervanche, 1980). Consequently, like race, the term ethnic could be in danger of losing its usefulness as a tool of analysis.

For our purposes, Schermerhorn's (1970: 12) definition of an ethnic group is adequate. It is: "A collectivity within a larger society having real or putative common ancestry, memories of a shared historical past, and a cultural focus on one or more symbolic elements defined as the epitome of their peoplehood." Schermerhorn suggests a considerable number of symbolic elements, e.g. kinship patterns, religious affiliation, nationality, language or dialect forms, which can be used singly or in combination as the bases of ethnicity. However, a necessary condition that must be present is "some consciousness of kind among members of the group" (ibid.).

A more contentious matter in the definition is the inclusion of phenotypical ("racial") features in the list of examples of symbolic elements. Opinion is split among theorists about the advisability of such an inclusion. The *Harvard Encyclopaedia of American Ethnic Groups* (Thernstrom, Orlov & Handlin, 1980) includes race in its long list of ethnic distinguishing characteristics (diacritica) but Smith (1982: 6ff) disagrees with this usage. He points out that there is a significant difference between phenotypical characteristics which are immutable — a person born with black skin cannot opt out of it, for example — and other ethnic diacritica, which an individual has liberty to choose. For similar reasons van den Berghe (1978: xv) has commented:

> "Precisely because a racial, phenotypical definition of group membership is far more stigmatizing than an ethnic definition, and typically gives rise to far more rigid social hierarchies, it is important to keep the analytical distinction clear."

A similar distinction is maintained throughout this book.

It should also be pointed out that the term ethnic *group* is an over-simplification that needs to be used with caution. In pluralist societies, people who identify with a particular ethnic common ancestry may not live in groups or enclaves, which include the degree of social organization and structure that the concept of group implies. To identify dispersed ethnics of this kind, Smith (1982: 2–6) has suggested the term *ethnic category*. This may lack many objectively identifiable ethnic diacritica, and rely more on shared subjective consiousness of its ethnicity and difference from other groups.

The racial and ethnic features found in pluralist societies are used as boundary markers by individuals and groups to distinguish themselves from other individuals and groups for the main purpose of maximizing individual or collective advantage in situations where competition occurs over access to scarce economic resources, social rewards, prestige and other kinds of valued "goods". These may all vary culturally and historically. What may be valued by one ethnic group may not be sought after by another: gold is of no use to a group of Inuit (Eskimos) in Canada unless they have access to shops, whereas it was eagerly sought by European miners. Historically, rubber was originally of little more than curiosity when Europeans first discovered and smuggled it out of the Amazon forests. It took the advent of the motor car and pneumatic rubber tyres to stimulate such demand for rubber that it became a highly valued commodity, and this in turn stimulated the exploitation of "inferior" native labour to first extract it and then work the rubber plantations that came to be established, under "superior" European management. A similar history could be traced in the case of the cotton plantations in the southern U.S.A.

Such relations between racial and ethnic groups can be analysed along lines suggested by the principle of *social closure*, first proposed by Max Weber (1968: 342) to analyse social class and other kinds of relations. As Parkin (1974: 3) explains:

> "By social closure Weber means the process by which social collectivities seek to maximize rewards by restricting access to rewards and opportunities to a limited circle of eligibles. This entails the singling out of certain identifiable social or physical attributes as the justificatory basis for exclusion. Weber suggests that virtually any group attribute — race, language, social origin, descent — may be seized upon provided it can be used for 'the monopolization of specific, usually economic opportunities . . . its purpose is always the closure of social and economic opportunities to *outsiders*'."

Techniques of exclusion entail the corollary of inclusion. That is, a group excludes others and symbolically marks this by emphasizing the undesirability or inferiority of one or another of their attributes, while including its own members and accentuating attributes which are held to be superior. Banton (1983: 10) has also suggested that "beliefs about race have mostly been used in processes of exclusion, [but] beliefs about ethnicity have been used to promote inclusion". However, this view may have lost sight of the fact that racial (phenotypical) attributes are being used increasingly by some groups such as West Indians in Britain, Afro-Americans in the U.S.A., and Aborigines in Australia as strategies of inclusion to develop group pride and identity. The concept of "Aboriginality" discussed in Chapter 4 of this book is one such example, and illustrates that what may be denigrated as an attribute by one ethnic group, may be positively valued by another. "Racial" features may be immutable in one sense, as one's membership of a group distinguishable by them is involuntary, but the way they are valued can change both culturally and over time.

Strategies of inclusion and exclusion can take many tangible forms, varying from actually denying members of "inferior" ethnic groups access to the institutions and organizations of "superior" groups, to depriving them of the knowledge needed to be able to operate successfully within such institutions. In the latter case the education system can be used as one means of recruiting new members for inclusion in one's own social or ethnic group and for excluding those that are not "fit" to belong. The English public school system is one example of this kind of control. Its result is to give one group considerable power or hegemony over the life chances of the other groups, be they distinguished on racial, ethnic, class or other grounds. A less obvious method of exclusion is "credentialism", which controls entry to valued types of employment by insisting that those who are admitted must obtain examination certificates (Miller, 1967). Although such a system appears to fit liberal ideas of justice by allowing persons to obtain employment on their individual merit and performance, the work of Bourdieu (1973) has shown that class and social inequalities can be reproduced through the education system and curriculum.

Although subordinate groups use their own processes of inclusion and exclusion, they can also employ a collective, reciprocal type of social closure to usurp a share of dominant groups' socio-economic resources. It is based on the power of "solidarism". As Parkin notes (1974: 10) "Solidaristic efforts are always directed at the usurpation of resources in the sense that claims to rewards, if successful, will normally result in some diminution of the share accruing to superordinate groups".

If we recall the definition of culture proposed in the first chapter, it seems feasible to maintain that some ethnic *groups* may develop cultures in the sense of survival programmes which include knowledge about practical inclusion and exclusion strategies. Whether ethnic *categories* also do so is open to question. Logically, the dominant or superior ethnic group possesses a more comprehensive and viable culture than other ethnic groups, and this enables it to exert hegemony over them. Groups distinguished on real or putative racial grounds may also maintain cultural survival programmes, but their status vis-à-vis the dominant group may be weaker as "inferior" cultures are linked to allegedly "inferior" physical attributes and correspondingly denigrated. This is not an invariable relationship. Jewish ethnic groups and categories have long been denigrated on spurious racial grounds, but have developed viable cultures which have proved eminently success-ful survival programmes and inclusion strategies, and have placed many Jews collectively and individually in positions of considerable power and influence. Other examples are Chinese groups in Malaysia, Japanese in Hawaii, and, latterly, Vietnamese in west-coast U.S.A. Each may have developed a cultural survival programme, in the face of opposition by the dominant group, to usurp a specialized "ecological niche" in a socio-economic sense, where phenotypical attributes carry little weight.

The function of ideologies of pluralism in race and ethnic relations

The cultures of racial and ethnic groups include beliefs and ideas about relationships with and the status of other groups. Where these are more or less systematized into coherent statements we can refer to them as ideologies. To avoid the contentious arguments that the concept of ideology can generate, the view is taken here that it can exist in the sense defined by Gould (1964: 315–6) as:

> "a pattern of beliefs and concepts both factual and normative which purport to explain complex social phe-nomena with a view to directing and simplifying socio-political choices, facing individuals and groups."

It is important for any argument to appreciate the force of the distinc-tion between factual and normative. An ideology can attempt to explain what is, as well as what ought to or should be achieved some time in the future. The two are frequently confused, thus, when politicians claim that Australia is a multicultural society it is rarely clear whether they mean now, in the 1980s, or if it will become so in years to come.

The geographical environment is no exception to being represented in ideological terms. In a very real sense the environment exists in people's minds as a taken-for-granted reality that is inevitably value-laden. For instance, the Australian outback means one thing to a grazier ("how many head of stock can it support"), another to a miner ("what minerals can be found there") and quite another to an Australian Aborigine ("this is where my totemic ancestors are located"). All three of these examples played a part in determining race relations between whites and Aborigines, as we shall see. Traditional but actually mythical ideas about the Australian bush and the types of social relationships it is supposed to have engendered form part of several ideologies in Australia, and are regularly invoked in times of crisis or danger.

Ideologies can operate in three ways according to Lepervanche (1980: 25). The first usage refers to "a whole system of beliefs and meanings that represent reality". People use such systems to make sense of the world and sanction existing social relations. The second usage brings in the notion of power and control. Here an ideology "can mean a system of meanings and values that project the interests of a particular class or group". Thus it can be a very powerful weapon of class domination and struggle, and many examples of this will emerge in what is described about race and ethnic relations in Australia. In this usage an ideology "can mystify social relations and constitute a system of illusory beliefs" (ibid.). The third usage of ideology, closely interrelated with the previous two usages, refers to the "general process of the production of meaning and ideas" (ibid.).

The second usage of ideology, i.e. its relationship to power and control, involves the concept of hegemony, and the whole social process together with the dominant political, social and cultural forces through which it is exercised (Marx, 1870: 21; Gramsci, 1971: 12–13; Williams, 1977: 55–71, 108–114; Lepervanche, 1980: 25). Hegemony can be maintained by the nation-state in a monocultural society, or by the dominant ethnic or racial group in a pluralist society, through power relationships arising out of the drive to maximize group advantage. At the same time, the dominant group legitimates its claims to power by the use of ideologies that attempt to influence the consciousness of dominated groups and delimit their access to power by means of various kinds of ethnic or racial boundary maintenance devices. In effect, actual political and economic hegemony is accompanied by what can be called ideological hegemony. The two operate on one another in a dialectical fashion characteristic of social life itself (Murphy, 1971: 117; Cohen, 1974: 13). If group relationships necessarily involve competition for scarce resources, rewards and prestige, then appropriate ideologies are needed to explain and justify such competitive behaviour and its consequences.

The hegemonic influence of an ideology can be maintained in a number of ways that provide a means of recognizing when hegemony has actually been achieved. The hegemonic ideology is clearly the dominant one despite the presence of competing counter-ideologies. It contains a variety of emotive parochial or nationalistic metaphors which virtually become common parlance in political claims or discussions about a society's pluralist characteristics. Examples are "The family of the nation" used to advocate multiculturalism in Australia, or the "cultural mosaic" in Canada. The hegemonic ideology employs "symbolic political language" or condensation symbols (Edelman, 1971: 2) such as "liberty", "equality". These are shorthand terms which stand in for a number of ideas and beliefs. There is also a constant working over and reformulation of the hegemonic ideology as power needs dictate, in the minds of people, through the mass media, education, and other kinds of "ideological state apparatuses" (Althusser, 1971). Lest it be thought that the evolution or formation of an ideology is an unproblematical business it must be kept in mind that mediation, resistance and contestation do occur with counter-ideologies vying with the hegemonic ideology.

Ideologies of pluralism, as I term them, are employed to legitimate relationships between racial or ethnic groups and members of the dominant society or "people of the State", i.e. *Staatsvolk*. Pluralist power relations and the nature of the pluralist society itself in which they occur can present to us at the level of empirical fact or at the level of ideology. The trick is to distinguish the nature of the dialectical relationship between the two. Armed with this theoretical framework, I now return to race and ethnic relations in Australia.

Race and ethnic relations from First Settlement to the end of the 1960s

Although Melanesian (Kanaka) labour was used in Queensland sugar plantations from the middle of the nineteenth century and generated race relations problems, historically it has been the Aborigines and Chinese which have been the major focus of attention. Discussion concentrates first on race relations between Aborigines and whites.

(a) Aborigines

The arrival of the First Fleet and start of settlement in New South Wales in 1788 brought an almost exclusively British force of white convicts, military and some few free settlers to the shores of Australia. As the other colonies of Victoria, South Australia, Western Australia, and Van Diemens Land (Tasmania) opened up, a similar pattern of first settlement emerged — convicts and military predominating over settlers. Estimates of the number of full-blood Aborigines on the continent at that time vary. The figure normally accepted is 250,000 in some 500 tribes (Elkin, 1954: 24–5). However, L. R. Smith (1980: 2–3) has made an estimate of 314,500 based on several sources. Figures such as these are somewhat suspect, as it was not until 1971 that Aborigines were counted in the Australian Census. Before then the Bureau of Census and Statistics adopted a very narrow interpretation of Section 127 of the Federal Constitution. This stated that "In reckoning the numbers of the people of the Commonwealth . . . aboriginal natives shall not be counted" (Yarwood & Knowling, 1982: 258–9). Since 1971, if a respondent to the Census is of mixed or racial origin he or she is asked how this ought to be identified.

Historically in the period up to the end of the 1960s, official policies, initially on the part of colonial governments, then State and

Federal governments, fall into three phases. These can be termed the pioneering phase, the segregation and protection phase, the assimilation phase, and vacillated over time between inclusion and exclusion policies.

(i) The pioneering phase — economic exploitation versus naive inclusion

The first phase lasted from initial settlement in 1788 to about the 1860s and the beginning of the gold rush. It was a period of pioneering, and frontier settlement mentality on the part of the white convicts, military and settlers faced with all the rigours of harsh climate and land. Inevitably they came into contact with Aborigines towards whom they showed extreme brutality stemming from "ignorance and callousness . . . [being] intent on exploiting economic opportunity in a land which had previously only shown ability to sustain life at virtually subsistence levels" (Stevens, 1970: 367). As settlers and their imported beasts spread over the land, Aboriginal needs and their inability to survive — partly due to the inherent conservatism of their cultures — clashed with the "entrenched economic interests" of the whites, and were disregarded (ibid.). Gradually the natives' habitat was destroyed by the white expansion and demands for grazing land. Contact between whites and Aborigines led to atrocities on both sides. White settlers' homesteads were burned, settlers were killed and their cattle speared, partly in retaliation for atrocities committed against Aborigines and partly because they were desperate for food. Stevens (1970: 368) considers that such contacts later in the period constituted a form of "pressure and response" rather than outright conflict. Other theorists, and more recently Aboriginal activists, claim that Aborigines adopted guerilla war tactics and in some cases put up stiff resistance to white invasions.[2]

Despite this, Aborigines were slaughtered in their thousands by methods ranging from paramilitary operations, like those used to exterminate the total population of Tasmanian Aborigines, to placing strychnine poison in flour provided by whites. Many events occurred well beyond official surveillance at the limits of frontier contact. However, many others took place with the full cognizance and even assistance of the law, coupled, in Stevens' view (1970: 371) with a policy of official detachment on the part of the authorities. In their view, shared by white settlers, expropriation of Aboriginal land was justified as they did not use it. This was probably inevitable in view of the polarized attitudes towards land discussed above.

However, nothing can condone the brutality which accompanied the seizure, though one can understand it when seen against the prevailing beliefs and ideas about Aborigines held by Europeans, particularly those in authority, and even by the church organizations and missionaries. These pose a curious paradox. On the one hand (Stevens, 1970: 370) Aborigines were portrayed as bestial, possessing every imaginable vice, and completely lacking any virtue, with "limited ability to respond to the higher orders of society introduced by Europeans". Aborigines were the most "debased race on the face of the earth" and constituted "the connecting link between man and the monkey tribes" (Turnbull, 1956: 123). On the other hand, Aborigines were fit to be civilized and Christianized by the church. As early as 1816 attempts were made to achieve this policy of inclusion largely through education, and they continued right up until at least the 1860s. As Rowley (1970: 19) has commented:

> "The attitudes of the first Australian governments were in
> a long tradition which illustrates both basic ethnocentricity
> and the best of intentions . . . [and] could be interpreted as
> an injunction to Christianize the heathen."

Not for the first time in the history of the British Empire did the church assume the role of a civilizing agent for Western colonialism. However, this sits oddly with another opinion expressed in May 1892 by the Secretary of the Aboriginal Protection Board of Western Australia to the Governor that "long-learned experience led inevitably to the conclusion that the European must efface the black race; the only question was with how little violence to humanity this effacement could be attended" (*Smoke Signals*, cited in Stevens, 1970). Needless to say, it clearly reflects European hegemony.

(ii) The segregationist and protectionist phase — physical exclusion

As a result of brutality and killings, coupled with disease and malnutrition, by the 1860s the Aboriginal population had been almost halved. Apart from those on urban fringes, the majority had been driven to the furthest extremities of the continent. It was evident that the government's benevolent policies of improving, civilizing, and advancing Aborigines through the Christian faith had failed. Worse, it seemed obvious that they were a dying race and doomed to inevitable extinction. Faced with failure on several grounds, the colonial governments retreated into despair and cynicism and adopted a different policy towards Aborigines.

This was to segregate and protect them in special reserves of land which were not required by European settlers. Such a policy had been advocated as early as 1845 by the Archbishop of Sydney at that time. It was also made advisable by pressure from the Colonial Office in London which was put on colonial governors to curb the worst excesses of the pastoral landowners. Various church missionary bodies intent on spreading the gospel — a form of ideological colonialism in itself — also became more active in Australia. All these moves led to the setting up of reserves and holding camps for Aborigines, on which they "were to be restrained for both their own protection and the racial purity of the broader community" (Stevens, 1970: 371). State-sponsored Aboriginal protection organizations were set up, with the first in Victoria (1860) and the last in the Northern Territory (1911). Segregation and protection were to continue until the outbreak of World War II, and were coupled with an almost complete lack of interest in Aboriginal education on the part of all governments.

The new policy was not entirely for the benefit of Aborigines, but represented a negative and clearly exclusive way of coping with what had become an intractable problem. The interference with economic growth produced by the confrontation between settlers and Aborigines, together with the government's inability to develop policies which would enable both sides to co-exist harmoniously, were at the root of the change. As Keith McConnochie (1981: 3) has commented, "Aboriginal affairs became embroiled in economic and political expediency, with the policies of protection and segregation offering a welcome release to politicians and settlers alike".

However, and possibly needless to say, these factors did not feature in the pluralist ideology employed to legitimate the new policy.

The ideology had three components, all of which lay the blame for the failure of the previous policy on Aborigines. The first component was the belief that they were a dying race faced with extinction. An appealingly humanistic parochial metaphor, "smooth the pillow", was invoked to demonstrate that negative protection was actually a humane way of allowing Aborigines to die in peace.[3] The second component was the firm belief that segregation was justified to avoid inter-breeding or miscegenation with Europeans, in order to preserve the purity of the European race. This fear of miscegenation was to become virtually a phobia in subsequent years and coloured official policies towards the Chinese. The third component, with particular bearing on education, was Social Darwinism. This entailed a fixed belief that the Aboriginal intellect was composed of base instincts, was incapable of higher mental processes. Thus there was no point in trying to encourage the development of Aborigines or educate them. So primitive were they, so the belief ran, that they had limited, if any, ability to adjust to the more advanced type of society introduced by the Europeans.

(iii) The assimilation phase — attempted official inclusion

As previously, the policy of segregation and protection did not succeed. Aborigines did not die out — indeed, by the early 1940s official estimates suggested that their numbers were increasing (Smith, 1980: 208). It was also apparent that governments had failed to provide adequate facilities and were actually discriminating against Aborigines by treating them as wards of the State. Reserves and settlements did little to provide Aborigines with the education and skills needed to move out and compete with Europeans. In consequence, the social and economic gap between the two communities was growing wider.

Ironically, by the 1930s and the increasing development of large pastoral cattle stations, especially in the Northern Territory and Queensland, it began to dawn on governments that Aborigines were an economic asset if not actually indispensable as stockmen. In 1937, the Commonwealth Government authorized a survey of economic conditions in the Northern Territory and cattle industry. This showed how essential Aborigines were to the cattle industry, and how dependent its future development was on an expanding, reasonably educated and reliable source of Aboriginal labour (Commonwealth of Australia, 1937). The survey's findings prompted the Minister for the Interior, with responsibility for the Northern Territory, the Hon. J. McEwen, to propose a policy in 1939 (McEwen, 1939) which would aim to reject previous restraints and coercion placed on Aborigines and call upon them to "share with us [the Europeans — interpolation added] the opportunities which are available in their own native land" (ibid., pp. 1–3). A new policy of assimilation was foreshadowed but its development was prevented by the outbreak of World War II.

After the war, assimilation was speedily adopted as official policy towards Aborigines by all States and the Commonwealth government, although it was not officially spelled out in clear detail until 1961, at the Native Welfare Conference (Rowley, 1972: 399). There the new policy was defined as follows, in terms that amount to an ideology of pluralism:

> "The policy of assimilation means that all Aborigines and part-Aborigines are expected eventually to attain the same manner of living as other Australians and to live as members of a single Australian community enjoying the same rights and privileges, accepting the same responsibilities, observing the same customs and influenced by the same beliefs, as other Australians."

Despite its apparent intent, the number of condensation symbols and amount of symbolic political language in that ethnocentric statement should be self-obvious. However, they were not unique as various State bodies had been issuing statements about the new assimilation policy since 1951. It was in September of that year that Paul Hasluck, Minister for Territories, had convened a meeting of State ministers and officials and informed them that the policy of protection had to be abandoned and assimilation adopted as the official goal. We need cite only one of many examples to illustrate how it was interpreted at the State level in those early days. In 1953 the Aborigines Welfare Board of New South Wales published a circular in which assimilation was interpreted as:

> "Resemblance, identity or conformity . . . it is the habits, attitudes, standards of living that really matter, and which

must conform before the community as a whole will accept
Aborigines on equal terms (in McConnochie, 1981: 7)."

Again, the ethnocentrism of the interpretation is quite obvious.

What circumstances really prompted such a remarkable *volte face*
in official thinking? This is a complex issue on which more research is
needed, but a number of interpretations can be advanced. Yarwood
& Knowling (1982: 259) suggest that the experiences of the War
affected Australian Aboriginal policy in three ways:

> ". . . by questioning the ideology of racism and race sup-
> pression, through the notoriety attached to Hitler's treat-
> ment of the Jews; by bringing Australian servicemen and
> Aborigines together, especially in the Northern Territory;
> and by creating an international community that found
> intolerable the mean, narrow and selfish prejudice which
> characterized Australia's treatment of Aborigines."

All these worthy factors may have played a part in stimulating a
new approach, but other reasons may have been equally cogent.
Hasluck introduced his new policy to the Australian Parliament on 8
June 1950 in a motion calling for a new deal for Aborigines. However,
he was not supported by the Prime Minister, Robert Menzies, who was
solidly ethnocentric, and the matter was not fully debated until the
debate on the Governor-General's speech in June 1951, when it became
a major issue. During the debate Australia's treatment of Aborigines
and work in the Trust Territory of Papua New Guinea were cited as
possible excuses which could be used by Russia and the Socialist
Eastern Bloc countries to "stimulate opposition to us among native
peoples throughout the Pacific area" (Commonwealth of Australia,
1951: 172). Strategic considerations operated in a Cold War atmos-
phere and dangerous international situation, so it was perceived by
those in power at the time. Improving the treatment of Aborigines
could be a possible way of countering such threats.

However, as in the past, economic influences played a major role.
In August 1952, Hasluck informed the House of Representatives that
the Aborigines had declining need of the huge reserves set aside for
them, as they were being attracted into mission stations and towns, and

to jobs provided by whites. Accordingly, the Northern Territory Government would be given permission to grant mineral exploration and mining rights. Aboriginal interests would be protected as they would benefit from the payment of royalties into an Aboriginal Trust Fund (Commonwealth of Australia, 1952: 45–7). We might note in passing how the whole issue was interpreted solely within a European economic framework, and how little Aborigines' sacred, custodial views towards the land were taken into account. In the 1970s these were to become the key questions underlying what came to be known as the land rights issue.

However, in 1952 they were not appreciated, and the interests of big business prevailed. In the debate prompted by Hasluck's proposal, Mr David Fairbairn explained that the government had three reasons for freeing the reserve land for mining. Vast bauxite deposits had been discovered off the coast of Arnhem Land, a prospector had found important deposits of silver, lead and zinc, which were being developed by the mining giant, Zinc Corporation of Broken Hill, and uranium had been discovered in the Northern Territory. "Surely it is not right", asked Fairbairn, "that our pioneers should have to run the risk of six months' imprisonment for prospecting on aboriginal reserves" (Commonwealth of Australia, 1952: 167). The emotive use of the condensation symbol "pioneers" should not need pointing out.

So matters developed apace in the 1960s. They gradually led to improved conditions for some Aborigines, and the 1966 decision by the Industrial Commission to grant them full award wages to be paid from December 1968, despite vigorous opposition from pastoralists. In 1967 a national referendum abolished Section 127 of the Constitution and gave the Federal Government power to legislate in respect of all Aboriginal affairs throughout Australia. In Yarwood & Knowling's opinion (1982: 262), to sum up this discussion of Aborigine white relations:

> "This was a period, therefore, of federal government encouragement to mineral prospectors in the Territory, of deliberately breaking down the old idea of an inviolable reserve in Arnhem Land, and bringing tribal Aborigines into touch with the white man's economy as the most

powerful agent of Western civilization. For this policy to
have its full effect, employment was indispensable, necessarily on the white man's award rates."

(b) The Chinese and Asians

I turn now to a briefer discussion of policies and ideologies of
pluralism in respect of Chinese and other Asians. Those already discussed in relation to Aborigines were attempts to cope with an indigenous racial problem. In one sense they were inclusive, i.e. they
had to include Aborigines in any consideration of Australia's future,
however limited, as there could be no possibility of shipping them out
of the country. In contrast, policies and ideologies of pluralism relating
to Chinese and other Asians (mostly Indians) were exclusive. In this,
the problem of Chinese could be and largely was shut out by gradually
restricting their activities and ultimately forbidding their entry into
Australia.

Chinese came to the country in the early part of the 1800s, fleeing
catastrophes in China. Initially they were brought in as indentured
labour to augment the dwindling number of convicts, and to work on
farms and rudimentary industries, where they were regarded stereo-
typically as a reliable and docile labour force. The discovery of gold in
the 1850s brought tens of thousands of Chinese into the country and
the goldfields, and into inevitable competition with white miners, the
"diggers". These protested that Chinese were unfairly working the
tailings, among other activities, and regularly followed up their grievances by physical assaults on Chinese. In 1855 the Victorian Government passed legislation restricting Chinese activities in the goldfields.
However, gold began to peter out, and they moved into other occupa-
tions, often as self-employed and independent businessmen, e.g. market gardening, small farming, pedlars, furniture making. They thus
stopped being a source of cheap, indentured labour and came into
further direct competition with whites.

A flood of discriminatory practices and legislation quickly followed, because it was claimed that Chinese were anti-working class
solidarity and unionism, a "servile and degraded class" (Johanson,

1962: 11). The Chinese Immigration Restriction Act was passed in Queensland in 1877 and was the start of a wave of colour conscious-ness. By the end of the century, Chinese had been "systematically restricted, contained and eventually excluded in the areas of agricul-ture, land-holding, mining, manufacture, right to vote, unionised labour and naturalisation" (Lepervanche, 1980: 26). In New South Wales, South Australia and Western Australia, factory legislation also restricted Chinese enterprise (Price, 1974).

These exclusive discriminatory measures were to prove long last-ing. For instance, right up until World War II, many of the industrial acts in Queensland demanded dictation tests in English, even where neither literacy nor knowledge of English were necessary for the industry (Ford, 1970: 105). It was not until 1967 that discriminatory clauses against the employment of Chinese labour were removed from industrial legislation in New South Wales. As Ford comments (ibid., p. 105), "Its purpose was to ensure Caucasian competitiveness in the industry".

Such economic reasons were often ignored in the pluralist ideology that evolved to justify anti-Chinese discrimination. In their place, blatantly racist ideas were used as the image of Chinese changed from that of a "good and faithful servant to the threatening bearer of all manner of moral diseases" (Lepervanche, 1980: 26, citing data from Evans et al., 1975: 261–262). Chinese "were portrayed as evil, lasci-vious, leprous creatures, fit for no white man's land" (ibid.). The ideology also invoked what was to be used later as a powerful conden-sation symbol during World War II to alert the nation against the imminent "yellow peril" of Japanese invasion. This was the threat Chinese in particular and Asians in general posed to the chastity of white women "whom Nature had entrusted with the instinct for racial purity" (Osborne, 1978: 115). Preservation of the "white race" and the phobia about miscegenation noted above in respect of Aborigines became a most powerful part of the debate that culminated in the Federal Immigration Restriction Act of 1901. During it the term White Australia was used frequently, and ultimately gave its name to the policy for which Australia became notorious.

Yet anti-Chinese discrimination was not the sole basis of its adop-tion — politicians of that time had a wider, ulterior motive. This was their efforts in the two decades prior to 1901 to work towards Australian nationhood and against imperial interference from Britain. Politicians of all persuasions were united against a common foe, despite earlier disputes, and used the notion of White Australia to bolster national consciousness, in what was an obvious exercise in ideological mystification. As Lepervanche comments (1980: 27):

">. . . the ideology of racial homogeneity and whiteness provided a powerful device for fostering support for Federation. In doing so it joined white labour to white capital and masked the conflicting interests between them which had been all too evident in the bitter industrial strife of the 1890s."

The White Australia Policy was adhered to for many years as the "indispensable condition of every other policy . . . firmly rooted in sentimental, economic and political ground" (Johanson, 1962: 24). Although its racist implications were played down in the 1930s and 1940s by apologetic excuses that Australia could obviously not assimilate Asians, it continued right through into the 1960s in one form or another. After World War II there was an increase in anti-Asian sentiment prompted by experiences of atrocities at the hands of the Japanese, and attempts to reduce anti-Asian discrimination were vehemently opposed by the Returned Servicemen's League (RSL), the Australian Natives Association, and even the Labor Government, and its Minister for Immigration, Arthur Calwell, who "pursued the 'White Australia' line with unrelenting consistency" (Johanson, 1962: 26). Calwell even deported a small number of Asians who had fled to Australia to escape the Japanese (ibid.).

The success of these exclusive measures can be judged from the fact that only 1,785 Asians were allowed into Australia between 1940 and 1960.[4] However, the policy was progressively opposed during the 1960s by churchmen, academics and other interested bodies. A series of ameliorative provisions were enacted, culminating in the reforms of March 1966 brought in by Hubert Opperman, Minister for Immigration in the Holt Liberal Government. The final, official demise of the policy occurred in 1975 with the passage through Parliament of the Racial Discrimination Act.

It would be tempting to see in this the result of counter-ideological pressure. However, the post-war period in Australia was a period of industrial and other economic expansion, fuelled by fears generated by Australia's long, undefended coastline, empty interior, closeness to Asia, and consequent need to "populate or perish". This emotive parochial metaphor was used to support the justification for the large-scale post-war immigration. This could not be sustained by drawing on traditional British migrants, then on European migrants, as by the end of the 1950s labour was needed in these areas too. Gradually the recognition was forced upon the government that sources of migrants outside traditional areas would have to be tapped, even from as far away as India and parts of non-Communist Asia. They too could provide labour with the kinds of skills needed in Australia. Australia's links with United States Pacific strategy meant an inevitable rapprochement with Japan, which in any case would come to provide an important market for Australian raw materials. Thus, for a variety of reasons the White Australia Policy and ideology were consigned to history. By the end of the 1960s the Federal Government was admitting approximately 10,000 non-European and part-European immigrants per annum "without incurring any significant outcry or generating any racial tensions" (Mackie, 1977: 10). After all, those were economic boom times!

(c) European, Caucasian immigrants

Historical analysis now turns to consider policies towards European immigrants. I can be brief as much of the scene has been set already. By Federation in 1901, and most certainly soon after it in the stirring events of World War I and creation of the ANZAC myth, an ideological image of Australian society had crystallized in the minds of politicians and most citizens. It was monolithic, Anglo-Saxon-Celtic-dominated, and white i.e. monocultural and monoracial. It was also chauvinistic, nationalistic and xenophobic (Kovacs & Cropley, 1975), thanks to the experiences of fighting for freedom from Britain, geographical isolation and ever-present phobias about the "yellow peril". However, a strong sentimental attachment to Britain, popularly invoked as the "mother country" or "home", continued. In any case all the major institutions of parliament, legal system, bureau-cracy, common language and education were modelled on British lines.

To this strange, British antipodean transplant were added some condensation symbols, amounting often to myths, that were peculiarly Australian, and served in time to influence policies towards immigrants. One myth was that of an egalitarian, classless society, shown to be empirically baseless by Encel (1970: 156–7). Such egalitarianism has tended to stultify intellectual and other kinds of excellence and lead to conformity and mediocrity. In schools, as McLaren (1968: 2) has commented, "this depressing jelly of philistinism is set in its mould by moral overtones of loyalty to the queen and country, worship of the flag, and reverence for the pioneers, the diggers and the sportsmen".

McLaren's acid comment alludes to other powerful condensation symbols and myths, namely the pioneers, the diggers and the sportsmen. Each of these was regularly held up as an ideal type to be emulated. Woe to those who obviously did not conform to the image or, worse, attempted to challenge it, for they were guilty of another heinous crime, namely "rocking the boat". This was as bad as "letting down one's mates", the product of a peculiarly Australian concept of classless mateship bred in a time of quasi-homosexual relationships between males in a frontier society lacking women. Strangely, it is still invoked today in times of crisis and danger such as war, or the 1983 bushfires in the state of Victoria.

All these myths and ideas had a profound effect on immigration policy. The ideology can be summed up by the term assimilation, and the policy by the term Anglo-conformism. These persisted in official thinking right up to the end of the 1960s with the "tenacity of an unchangeable dogma" (Kovacs & Cropley, 1975: 119). It affected the intake of immigrants especially during the period prior to World War II. British were preferred because it was thought that they would fit in easily, i.e. conform. Non-British immigrants were discouraged, as happened in the case of Italians after 1925 (Jupp, 1966: 6). Even some Jewish refugees in 1938 to 1940 were strongly opposed by the conservative element in politics. The term "reffo" was coined to refer to them at the popular level, and this continued to be used about non-Jewish refugees who came into the country after the war.

It seems abundantly clear that Anglo-Celtic hegemony underlay the strong assimilationist ideology which persisted until the 1960s and produced for migrants only a few measures to help them assimilate easily. In education at least, it was more a case of letting the new arrivals sink or swim. As Martin has pointed out (Martin, 1976b: 2), such bodies as the Commonwealth and state bureaucracies, political parties, trade unions, churches and voluntary bodies were, overall, indifferent to the migrant presence.

> "This indifference was based on the conviction that the success of migrant adaptation depended 'not on structures and policies, but on the goodwill of *individual* migrants and *individual* Australians' and 'that it would be contrary to the prevailing egalitarian values and detrimental to assimilation for migrants, as migrants, to be given unique privileges or consideration of any kind' (Martin, 1972: 14)."

Here we see the egalitarian myth about Australian society used to justify policy.

Even though the availability of British migrants declined in the late 1950s and 1960s, and Australia was forced to take others from Southern and Eastern Europe, the policy of Anglo-conformism continued, backed by the assimilationist ideology. Some shift in policy can be detected in the late 1960s but even in 1967 the Minister for Immigration, Bill Snedden, could still state publicly (Snedden, 1969):

> "We must have a single culture — if immigration implied multi-cultural activities within Australian society, then it was not the type Australia wanted. I am quite determined we should have a monoculture, with everyone living in the same way, understanding each other, and sharing the same aspirations. We don't want pluralism."

Within barely ten years Snedden's statement would appear blatantly discriminatory, so great were the changes brought in by the 1970s. They would completely reverse Snedden's image of society and generate another ideology of pluralism, to justify the evolving policies that were virtually forced on the government by increasing numbers of immigrants. Tracing these continues the theme that has been developed in this analysis, namely the interaction between the hegemony exercised by the dominant Anglo-Celtic majority over Aboriginal, Chinese and European immigrant minorities, and the ideologies of pluralism used to legitimate it. In many instances the exercise of power relationships was far from subtle, and amounted in the extreme case of Tasmanian Aborigines to blatant genocide. Deprivation of land, outright conflict, racial harassment and persecution, discriminatory legislation and restrictive trade practices were only a few of the strategies used by the Anglo-Celtic *Staatsvolk* to preserve their economic, political and social power and influence. It extended into all the major institutions of the society, and, in any case, these were modelled on British lines and thus were inherently ethnocentric and inclusive.

As the economic and political needs of the Anglo-Celtic majority changed through time, so did their processes of exclusion and inclusion, as best illustrated by the three phases policies towards Aborigines underwent. At the same time various metaphors and myths were invoked as part of the evolving ideologies of pluralism which justified exclusion and bolstered the inclusion of whites only within the same Anglo-Celtic or British majority, or of Aborigines on terms that were clearly favourable to Anglo-Celtic economic gain. Despite the *de jure official* rhetoric that has preached assimilation of Aborigines, at the *grass-roots* level of everyday social relationships between whites and Australia's blacks, *de facto* exclusion of the latter has prevailed as Chapter 4 illustrates. In contrast, policies and ideologies towards Chinese and other Asians were obviously exclusive and continued so right up until the demise of the so-called White Australia Policy.

Policies and ideologies towards British or fellow Anglo-Celtic immigrants were obviously inclusive — they were expected to "fit in" as speedily as possible, though little official effort was made to assist this process. In consequence even these additions to the Australian population did not originally gain access to the socio-economic rewards, resources and prestige enjoyed by the established Anglo-Celtic majority. However, they had a far better chance than the non-British immigrants, whose numbers began to dominate the settler intake by the 1960s, eventually coming to outnumber those arriving from the "motherland". This growing imbalance, and the flood of non-British, even Asian, immigrants in the 1970s posed a clear threat to Anglo-Celtic hegemony. How it was countered is the subject of the next chapter.

Notes to Chapter 2

1. Anglo-Celtic, rather than "British" or "Anglo-Saxon", seems the most accurate term to describe the origins of the largely British, Scottish and Irish immigrants (both free and convicted) who made up the first waves of settlers in Australia. The term is being increasingly used in the literature.
2. Substantiated by Aboriginal members of the Aboriginal Research Centre, Monash University. Stevens (1970: 368) cites numerous references to support these and other details. See also Gale & Brookman (1975).
3. Interestingly, the same metaphor was used by the British about Maoris in New Zealand.
4. Even this figure is an inflated one as it includes White Russians and Eurasians in the category of "Asians".

3 Development of cultural pluralism

The impact of post-Second World War mass immigration on Australian ethnic groups[1]

The strong assimilationist ideology relating to immigrants into Australia that was still firmly entrenched in both official and popular thinking until the end of the 1960s had hegemonic consequences throughout the whole society. I have suggested in the previous chapter that hegemony can present in at least two ways. The first is the actual control by the majority group over the minority group's life chances, i.e. their access to an equitable share of socio-economic rewards and resources, possibilities to realize their potential for self-actualization and satisfaction. Denial of these by the majority group is clearly discriminatory. The second is ideological hegemony. This is the ideological legitimation or justification of the differential power relationships between majority and minority groups.

Prior to the 1970s in Australia there is no doubt that both kinds of hegemony were operating, together with the dialectical relationship between them. Considerable empirical evidence can be brought to support this (e.g. Storer, 1975; Martin & Cox, 1975; Jabukowicz & Buckley, 1975; Martin, 1976a & b; Ford, 1974). Migrants were discriminated against in industry, law, social welfare, education and other areas of the economic and socio-political system. Concurrently the ideology of assimilation was promoted assiduously by government and semi-government agencies of all kinds, to ensure that immigrants "fitted in" and learned acceptable Australian ways. This attitude was often used by trade unions to ensure that "money-hungry" migrants did not work long periods of overtime or work hard and thus break down union-won conditions — Australians not being noted for exces-

47

sive devotion for hard work. Thus one finds the comment of the Secretary of the Queensland branch of the Australian Workers Union (the largest union in the Commonwealth) to the press in January 1958 (Ford, 1970: 108):

> "They [migrants] are breaking down our conditions . . .
> There would be 200 in Brisbane now for compensation with
> crook backs. If you shouted 'fire' they would move in no
> time. In one instance a car load of migrants who were
> refused jobs because they did not have a union ticket paid
> $28 for a taxi to get tickets . . . *It is time they learnt our
> ways*" [my emphasis].

This illustrates a number of common beliefs about migrants that verge on racism. That migrants suffer from "crook backs" (strained back muscles) excessively is a common stereotype in industry and even the medical profession and hospitals. The assertion that migrants could nonetheless afford a taxi fare to Townsville to get tickets implies that they are exploiting the compensation system ("bludging on their mates" in the Australian idiom). It is conveniently forgotten that Australians frequently bludge on fellow Australian workers. The final sentence, "It is time they learnt our ways", is both assimilationist and arrogantly ethnocentric.

In a wider sense the ideology of assimilation and exclusive policies adopted to promote Anglo-conformism can be interpreted as ways of maintaining the whole existing social order and its Anglo-Celtic-dominated power relationships. As Foster (1981: 310) has suggested:

> "The ideology of assimilation was used to ensure that
> migrants did not challenge the cultural identity of Australian
> society or the existing class structure. It was also promoted
> by governments in order to ensure the favourable response
> of the Australian public to the immigration policy. Thus it
> helped legitimate the consequences of a policy which might
> in practice have worked against the interests of some
> Australian, as well as immigrant, groups."

A corollary of the assimilation ideology should be noted. The whole process was assumed to be the responsibility of the migrant as an individual to achieve the political and legal transformation to an "Australian" and to assume a new self-identity and social status position as a "new Australian". Failure to do so was attributed to some deficiency in the individual and conveniently exonerated the government from blame if the assimilation did not occur. By the mid-1960s it was clear that the policy was not succeeding, and we can now attempt to trace what evolved in its place. By way of illustration particular attention will be given to the education system because, however limited its response to the migrant presence, it has attempted to make some changes to schooling practices and curricula to meet the pressures generated by increasing numbers of children in schools. In addition, the education system has attempted to carry out its function of one of Australia's "ideological state apparatuses" (Althusser, 1971) and adapt to the convolutions of changes in the ideology of pluralism from time to time. In doing so it has assisted with the process of hegemonic control, through its strategic role in the management and dissemination of knowledge. As Gramsci has observed (1971: 350): "Every relationship of 'hegemony' is necessarily an educational relationship". So it can be shown in Australia.

Schooling, culture, curriculum and power

In Musgrave's (1965: 124) view, the education system performs five social functions: the transmission of a society's culture, the provision of innovators who might contribute to changes in various spheres of life, the training of future leaders and the inculcation of loyalty to existing forms of government, the selection and sorting of the oncoming population into the existing hierarchical structures of the society, and, finally, the qualifying of young people to take their place in the workforce structured by the society's needs, at its present and future stages of development. These functions are clearly not exclusive — the ideological function is overlooked, for example — but they do serve to draw attention to the close links between the education system and some of the bases of power and control in society. Such a view has become commonplace in recent years in the sociology of education. In short, the education system functions to reproduce the existing hierarchical status arrangements in society and perpetuate inequalities in power and control (Bernstein, 1971; Young, 1971; Bourdieu & Passeron, 1977). The education system also functions to reproduce the existing cultural order, and ensure its continuity, thus contributing to the wider dialectical relationship between cultural control and its distribution on the one hand, and economic and political stratification on the other (Williams, 1973: 3–16).

It should be apparent that the education system has the capacity to be hegemonic in several ways. Not only does it process pupils, stamping them into a mould (if one wants to adopt the factory metaphor favoured in the 1960s), and fitting them for a place in the workforce, but it also processes knowledge, selecting that which confirms the social and cultural order, and rejecting most opposing views and alternative cultural orders. The education system also maintains hegemony, in Apple's (1979: 5) opinion, by recreating a world-view and related social relations that benefit the dominant groups in a society. As suggested in Chapter 2, following Weber, the dominant groups need not be distinguished by their class or status affiliations, with which so much of the above social or cultural reproduction theory is concerned, but may be distinguished on ethnic grounds. In short, the dominant ethnic group in a society can exert hegemony through the education system, and thus ensure that the inequalities between it and other ethnic groups are reproduced. Further, following Apple's (ibid.) and Gramsci's contention that hegemony "saturates" people's very consciousness, such inequalities between ethnic groups may be so masked and concealed, that their full extent is not appreciated.

The curriculum in schools functions as the major vehicle for processing knowledge and creating hegemony. I define it as a *selection* from a society's public stock of valued traditional and current knowledge and conceptions, usually *organized* purposefully by such enculturation agencies as schools, and *transmitted* to pupils in such conventional subdivisions as syllabuses and units. All three stages of selection, organization and transmission provide opportunities for schools to exert direct control over the life chances of children from ethnic backgrounds as I have discussed elsewhere (Bullivant, 1982a). Bernstein goes further and in a celebrated passage identifies other dimensions of "knowledge processing" that provide opportunities for controlling power (Bernstein, 1971: 47):

"How a society selects, classifies, distributes, transmits and evaluates the educational knowledge it considers to be public, reflects both the distribution of power and the principles of social control."

Such a view is neatly caught by Foucault's (1977) "knowledge-power". This conjunction highlights the close relationship between these two features of social life.

The concept of "educational knowledge" is too broad to be really useful in the analysis attempted below. It is conceptually appropriate to adopt the conventional division used by anthropologists to distinguish between instrumental knowledge and expressive knowledge. The former concerns technical knowledge that is intended for use in enabling people to generate and interpret social behaviour, interact with others, learn appropriate skills for future status-roles in the workforce and so on. Such knowledge-for-use or in-use seems closely related to achieving one's life chances as Melvin Tumin has pointed out (Tumin, 1977).

Expressive knowledge, on the other hand, is that which is related to the expressive side of culture, in terms of aesthetic pursuits, creative arts, literature, religion, and socio-cultural values. Although there can be some overlap between this kind of knowledge and instrumental knowledge, the expressive variety seems more closely related to a person's lifestyle. The risks involved in making this kind of simple distinction are obvious, but it seems worthwhile to do so, if only for heuristic purposes that will become apparent later.

Identifying those who exercise hegemonic control through schooling and the curriculum is no easy task. Teachers, public officials in the educational bureaucracy, and members of school boards stand in the front rank of those involved with knowledge management. They are usually members of the dominant social class or ethnic group, and inevitably reflect its vested interests in what and how they teach. They may be unaware of the strength of this hegemonic influence, so profoundly can their consciousness be "saturated" by the hegemonic ideology. On the other hand, they may be aware of what they are doing, a situation that is most likely to arise when teachers and other front-rank knowledge managers have limited discretionary powers and autonomy, due to being part of a centralized education system as is the case in Australia. There, control of the public or government school sector, catering for approximately 78 per cent of primary and secondary level enrolments, is the responsibility of each of the six States plus the Northern Territory, and their respective educational bureaucracies. The remaining 22 per cent of enrolments are catered for by Independent denominational schools, historically modelled on the Scottish and Arnoldian public school tradition, though now well Australianized, and by the Catholic systemic schools.

The Federal Government plays no *direct* part in the day-to-day running of the education system, but exercises *indirect* influence over all schools through its major bureaucratic and ideological arm, the Schools Commission. This advises the Federal Government on the needs of government and non-government schools, the necessity for and conditions of financial assistance, and the allocations to be granted out of Treasury funding. The Schools Commission also issues regular triennial reports which play a major role in influencing thinking about future directions of Australian education and the desirable emphases for curriculum change and development. It has been at this level that ideology-making about education has been most obvious (see, for example, Schools Commission Interim Committee, 1973).

The State school systems in particular and the Catholic systemic schools to a lesser degree have borne the brunt of educating immigrant children. Until the mid-1970s, and even today in some States, the curriculum planning has been centrally controlled by each State's bureaucracy, but also influenced to some degree by other interest groups such as universities, teachers' unions, and subject associations. Moreover, the curriculum in secondary schools is over-responsive to the demands of examinations at Grade 12 (Form 6), despite some liberalization in some States since the late 1970s. Other Federal bodies such as the Canberra-based Curriculum Development Centre and the Education Research and Development Committee have exercised some influence over decisions to free-up the curriculum.[2]

Control over immigrant education is thus many layered, extending from Federal level, where ideological considerations have been extremely influential, down to the school level where knowledge management has been the main concern. However, as we shall see, at the latter level ideological considerations have also been apparent.

Pluralist ideologies and educational responses in the 1960s

Let us begin by briefly reviewing education in the 1960s. The assimilationist ideology and Anglo-Conformist policies that persisted until the end of the period generated an educational response for immigrant children that was virtually nil: an Anglo-dominated curriculum and selection of knowledge was the norm. Children of ethno-cultural backgrounds were more or less left to sink or swim, to "pick up English" and an understanding of Australian culture without the aid of special provisions. Thus the necessity to select special kinds of knowledge and experiences for the curriculum scarcely arose. Instead, immigrant children were seen as a problem in the classroom: their movements were unpredictable as they tended to arrive unexpectedly, they disrupted normal teaching work, and were unfamiliar with English. Although there was some quickening of interest among some teachers in the education of these children in the mid- and late-sixties, it was still in ways that were Anglo-conformist, teacher-dominated and assimilationist. As Martin comments of this period (Martin, 1976b: 13), "the pre-eminence of the teachers' definition of the situation was mostly taken for granted".

The educational bureaucracy and administrators in each State were unable and largely unwilling to assist teachers' attempts to cope with the problems of immigrant children. Various committees of inquiry were set up, but under such terms of reference and using such dubious statistical procedures, that their findings were virtually useless, and either ignored or concealed the problems. These tactics enabled information that ran counter to Anglo-conformist official policies and ideologies to be screened out and excluded from the public agenda of concern. Such control of information about the true state of affairs in schools, and teachers' inability to cope with mounting migrant numbers, even extended to State departments refraining from collecting adequate data on the distribution of migrant pupils, their knowledge of English, their scholastic performance and their learning and psychological difficulties (Martin, 1976b: 19). This hegemonic policy was even

justified by Dr Wyndham, the Director General of Education in New
South Wales, when addressing an Australian Citizenship Convention in
1963 (Commonwealth Department of Immigration, 1963: 21):

> "We deliberately refrain from collecting any statistics in re-
> gard to school pupils from overseas. Once they are enrolled in
> school, they are, from our point of view, Australian children."

The assimilationist assumptions are quite obvious. Less apparent, but
nevertheless present as a "hidden agenda", is the fact that rational
curriculum decision-making is effectively inhibited when the numbers
of pupil clients for whom it is intended are not available.

The image of a monocultural, and by extension monolingual
Australia, had as a corollary that the society should be white, i.e.
monoracial. This was a result of the hegemonic White Australia Policy
that excluded Asians from the country for barely concealed economic
reasons and spurious racial purity, and lingered on in official thinking
until the late 1960s. The image was reflected in the curriculum. There
was almost total disregard of Asian geography, history and politics.
Africa was almost completely ignored. What was taught about these
regions consisted of depersonalized geography that concentrated on
physical and commercial aspects, with little attention being paid to the
human side of the continents. A further tendency in geography and
social studies was to concentrate on topics, such as "small communities
of Asia", that implicitly stressed regions of backwardness, poverty, and
lack of economic development. In the place of Asia and Africa, most
syllabuses at the secondary level concentrated on American, British and
especially Australian geography and history. A survey of social studies
syllabuses in all secondary schools carried out in 1967 by a research team
at the Australian Council for Educational Research (Bennett, 1968)
found that "in history, almost two-thirds of the material over all grades
and in almost all grades separately [were] devoted to British and
European history, but only five per cent of the total time [was] devoted
to Asian, South-East Asian, or Pacific history" (Dufty, 1970: 13).

Changes in ideology and education in the 1960s

It was abundantly clear by the mid-1960s that immigrants were not
assimilating and were even making increasingly vocal demands to have

their cultures recognized. In addition their numbers increased dramatically. Between 1950 and 1970 about 2.5 million migrants entered Australia, helping to lift the population from 7.5 million in 1947 to 12.5 million in 1969 (Yarwood & Knowling, 1982: 284). More than half the migrants were non-British, and as the British migrant flow diminished, the European and even non-European, non-Caucasian flow increased to take its place. At successive Australian Citizenship Conventions commencing in the late 1950s, migrants made repeated requests to have the policy of assimilation abandoned, but with little immediate success (Harris, 1979). It was not until the mid-1960s that a new ideology began to be referred to in official circles, at first cautiously, then more explicitly. This was the ideology of integration that attempted to accommodate what had virtually been forced upon the government, namely, that migrants had an important contribution to make and should not have to abandon their cultures.

The new ideology was even given bureaucratic recognition in structural terms with the creation of an Office of Migrant Integration within the Ministry of Immigration. Its first Officer-in-Charge of Integration, John Rooth, wrote in 1968: "We should not merely tolerate but also respect and, on occasions, encourage cultural differences . . . As members of minority groups they [the migrants] can make invaluable contributions to our Australian way of life while retaining their ethnic identity" (Rooth, 1968: 61). The Minister for Immigration, Phillip Lynch, was more rhetorical when speaking at the 43rd Annual Summer School organized by the University of Western Australia in 1970 and devoted to Australia's immigration policy (Lynch, 1972: 10):

> "The earlier desire to make stereotype Australians of the newcomers has been cast aside. The use of the word 'integration' instead of 'assimilation' is not mere semantics — it is the outward sign of a fundamental change in attitude of the Australian government and people."

It is worth recalling that only one year earlier, Phillip Lynch's predecessor, the Minister for Immigration, Bill Snedden, had warned in a newspaper article: "I am quite determined that we should have a monoculture, with everyone living in the same way, understanding each other, and sharing the same aspirations. We don't want pluralism" (Snedden, 1969). His statement is all the more remarkable as integration was already being implemented by 1967 and was being advocated by prominent public figures even earlier at Australian Citizenship Conventions. For example, in 1965, Sir John Allison, speaking at that year's convention, appealed to Australians to preserve what was best in their own traditions but also adopt the best of what migrants could offer Australia. The aim of such an inclusive policy would be to "create in the Southern Hemisphere a united nation of nations with all that is best in European culture and traditions — a Europe of the sun, without national barriers and with a common citizenship" (cited in Harris, 1979: 31).

However, the education system was slower to respond to the new ideology, despite the rhetoric in which it was couched and the appeal of its symbolic political language or condensation symbols such as "united nation of nations", "Europe of the sun", and so on. Indeed, the regularly reiterated appeals of Australian Citizenship Conventions between 1962 and 1970 to include more European content in school syllabuses for all children to learn were virtually ignored. In Harris's (1979: 33) opinion this was indicative of how little notice the education system took of such suggestions, to place more emphasis on languages, history, geography, arts and cultures of European nations. However, there were some slight changes by the early 1970s when some of the more exotic aspects of the major migrant lifestyles began to appear in some primary school syllabuses — dancing, customs, costumes, ethnic foods and so on — but really extending little further than tokenism, being additives on to the curriculum rather than a complete reorganization of it.

One official innovation occurred in 1970 with the introduction of the Child Migrant Education Programme by the Commonwealth Government. It resulted in the provision of special English classes in schools and the employment of teachers as migrant-teacher aides. How much of this was a belated recognition of structural changes and strains induced by increased migrant numbers, or a response to an ideological shift is uncertain. In Lois Foster's opinion it enabled the government to restrict "the definition of child migrant education to the teaching of English [and] enabled migrant problems to be defined in isolation from 'mainsteam' education policy. This was a clear result of the operation of an assimilationist ideology" (Foster, 1981: 310–11). Similarly, Martin (1976b; 1978: 113–45) has provided evidence that even though some expansion of educational facilities occurred in the early 1970s the early strategy of assimilating migrant children by teaching them English was not abandoned altogether, but further possibilities were added instead, especially bilingual education and community languages. Even later ideas of multicultural education and ethnic schooling did not replace the teaching of English. To this extent, the assimilationist ideology and related educational policies remain with us, as evidence of continued hegemonic control over the curriculum.

The 1970s — towards multiculturalism

Educational developments in schools and curriculum were in the doldrums for the first few years of the 1970s, even though official inquiries and programmes began to expand. The Immigration (Education) Act was passed by the Liberal Commonwealth Government in 1971 to provide support more for adult than child education. The latter was catered for by increased provisions in the Child Migrant Education Programme, where the emphasis was beginning to shift from the elementary English teaching, towards catering for the broader problems of migrant children's education. In 1974 the Inquiry into Schools of High Migrant Density in New South Wales and Victoria was held and provided evidence that "the usual school programs are designed for Australian children and make no concessions to the particular needs and backgrounds of migrant pupils" (Australian Department of Education, 1975: 6). In Martin's opinion, the schools were continuing to function in a "narrow assimilationist mould" and were staffed by teachers who "were not adequately prepared to work in schools [with high migrant populations] and there was much indifference and even intolerance towards migrant children" (Martin, 1976b: 29). There were some exceptions, of course, among teachers and a few educationists in colleges and university faculties of education. The latter were guided by a variety of theoretical approaches ranging from the ideas of intercultural education, then fashionable in the United States, to compensatory and cultural deprivation education — the "political arithmetic" sociology of education — also current in the States and

Great Britain. Multicultural education was being proposed by some academics in teacher training courses and journal articles (e.g. Bullivant, 1972; 1973a, b), but in general most teacher training emphasized teaching of English as a second or foreign language, thus contributing to the continuation of an assimilationist ideology.

The election of the Whitlam Labor Government at the end of 1972 generated structural changes in the education system with the setting up of the Australian Schools Commission. Its Interim Committee (1973) published its first report, *Schools in Australia*, in May 1973. It contained a scant 11 lines on migrant Education (Schools Commission, 1973: 107), prefaced by the comment that, "The Committee has not been able to undertake a detailed investigation into the education of migrant children". Recommendations for this area of need were wedded firmly to the then highly influential ideology of providing compensatory education for the disadvantaged. The Commission also followed trendy overseas thinking emanating from socialist theorists in Britain, particularly the Open University, to advocate that one could radically alter the structure of Australian society through educational means. This was to launch teacher training and some teacher unions into a disastrous period of militancy and radicalism, which lasted throughout the 1970s, and from which education is only just emerging. After years of Liberal Government mismanagement and bolstering of privilege in Australia, such ideas caught the imagination of education-ists and, in any case, were in tune with the general ideological ground-swell of the Australian ethos which has stressed the egalitarian nature of the society since Federation in 1901, however mythical this is in reality (Encel, 1970: 156–7).

Of probably greater impact on education, groping in the dark, as it were, for some light to illuminate thinking about migrant education, were the ideas of the new Minister for Immigration and Ethnic Affairs in the Whitlam Government, the Hon. A. J. (Al) Grassby. He is a flamboyant figure with considerable oratorical powers and, probably more than any other individual, has played a major role in shaping thinking about migrants and migrant education in Australia. His first statement (Grassby, 1973a) appeared in a small pamphlet entitled *A Multi-cultural Society for the Future*, and is most notable for containing all the kinds of symbolic political language, condensation symbols, myths and metaphors that one associates with an ideology (Edelman, 1971, 1977; Barthes, 1973). Australia must become "a family of the Nation" and offer "equal opportunity for all". Australia's "national fabric" has been woven from "rather ill-assorted strands" (a weaving metaphor that is very common in the rhetoric of pluralism) to become one of the "most cosmopolitan societies on earth". A spate of publications followed (Grassby, 1973b, 1974a, b, c) from this energetic publicist, but it was probably his first statement that had the greatest impact.

Educationists seized on the concept of multicultural Australia as a rallying point for their ideas, even though it was little understood, to judge from the discussions at a National Seminar for Teacher Educators on "The Multi-Cultural Society", held at Macquarie University, Sydney, in August 1974. The concepts of pluralism and multiculturalism baffled most participants, the opening speech, read *in absentia* by a representative of the Minister for Education, antagonized those present and gave a remarkably simplistic view of multicultural education. In the Minister's opinion it ought to include "something of the religion, the literature and the history of migrant peoples . . . The treasures of the Renaissance in Italy, the story of the liberation of Greece, the music of Austria, the art of Holland may possibly become as intellectually exciting to Melbourne teachers as the pigskin folk festival Collingwood versus Footscray" (National Seminar for Teacher Educators, 1974: 38). Despite these and similar ideas which characterized proceedings, some positive recommendations were adopted at the seminar, but they were included in the existing framework of schooling and curriculum and their assumptions, and did not significantly challenge them. After this, numerous conferences were launched during the remainder of the 1970s, but no unanimity developed about coping with migrant education. The situation in New South Wales described by Young (1977) was typical of the whole of Australia at that time, being characterized by five major, overlapping components: multicultural programmes emphasizing the exotic aspects of migrant cultures, ethnic studies programmes emphasizing the histories and countries of origin of migrant groups, community language programmes, bilingual programmes, English as a second language programmes.

One can detect two major emphases in the curriculum of this period. The first, and by far the most common, "was to focus on aspects of 'ethnic cultures' which fitted in with existing ideas about worthwhile knowledge [to be selected and organized — my interpolation], by stressing aspects of 'ethnic cultures' harmonious with the existing educational process or different in acceptable ways: this approach emphasized safe, neutral aspects of cultural pluralism, such as music, food preferences and cooking habits, traditional (folk) culture and religious observances" (Martin, 1976c). The second approach, adopted by very few educators, was more phenemonological and challenged the assumption that Western knowledge was paramount and immutable, and learned primarily through intellectual understanding (Martin, 1976c; Young, 1977: 3; Bullivant, 1975a, b). What was not challenged about the curriculum, apart from an academic critique by a few social scientists (e.g. Bullivant, 1976; Martin, 1976c, 1978; Wiseman, 1974), was its relationship to the power structures of society.

Even the Schools Commission's thinking, radical and innovative as it was, did not fully come to grips with this aspect of the problem, though it did adopt the new multicultural ideology without reservation in its *Report for the Triennium 1976–78*, published in 1975. The chapter on The Education of Migrant Children opens with the confident claim, "Australia is a multicultural society", but then advocates measures that follow the neutral and acceptable approach to educating such children (Schools Commission, 1975: 125):

> ". . . the *multicultural reality* of Australia needs to be reflected in the school curricula — languages, social studies, history, literature, the arts and crafts — in staffing and in school organization. While these changes are particularly important to undergird the self-esteem of migrant children they also have application for all Australian children growing up in a society which could be greatly enriched through a wider sharing in the variety of *cultural heritages* now present in it [emphasis added]."

Other committees established after Grassby's first pronouncement on multicultural Australia adopted an approach similar to the Schools Commission's. For example, the Committee on the Teaching of Migrant Languages in Schools, set up in November 1974 by the Labor Government, opens with the assertion, "Australia is a cultural mosaic" — and proceeds to advocate a number of worthwhile measures. These were a distinct improvement on contemporary practices, but did not significantly challenge the whole imbalance of the curriculum and its emphasis on reproducing Anglo-conformist structures and power domination.

For some committees and organizations, adopting the multi-cultural ideology can be interpreted as little more than bandwaggon-ing. For example, the Victorian Association of Teachers of English as a Second Language became the Victorian Association for Multicultural Education, but did not change its approach to the curriculum. It still advocated the teaching of English as a second language to migrant children and adults, and children's first language maintenance in schools. Little or no account is taken of the need to cater for all children and wider issues in the curriculum, that might reflect the notion of multicultural Australia implied by the organization's new title.

Meanwhile more structural changes occurred at the Common-wealth level. The responsibility for migrant education was transferred in June 1974 from what was known in those days as the Department of Labour and Immigration to the Department of Education. Labour and Immigration were split to form two new Ministries, of which the new Department of Immigration and Ethnic Affairs assumed direct responsibility for all matters pertaining to migrants. These changes were not insignificant as they marked the end of a period in which migrants were seen as sources of labour for an expanding economy — factory fodder to be compulsorily drafted where required in Australia — and the beginning of realization at the official level that by the 1970s migrants made up a sizeable proportion of the general population. However, as Martin's (1978) analysis of labour and union relations indicates, such thinking was not apparent on the factory floor and in industry generally. There, migrants were still regarded as cheap labour and associated with lower paid, manual jobs, many of which Anglo-Australians did not want to do.

With the change of government following the dismissal of Whitlam in 1975 there is evidence of some revisionist thinking in the Departments of Education and Immigration and Ethnic Affairs, with mention of integration appearing in official statements, by the Ministers for Education and Immigration respectively (Carrick, in Bostock, 1977: 135–38; MacKellar, 1976, 1978). The latter in particular hark back to thinking that was current in the mid-1960s, even to the extent of implying that the White Australia Policy had not been abandoned fully. In his Ministerial Statement to Parliament on Immigration Policies and Australia's Population (MacKellar, 1978: 2–3) the Minister stated:

> 3. The size and composition of migrant intakes should not jeopardize social cohesiveness and harmony within the Australian community.

> 2. Immigration policy should be applied on a basis which is non-discriminatory . . . [and] consistently to all applicants regardless of their race, colour, nationality, descent, national or ethnic origin or sex . . .

> 9. Policies governing entry and settlement should be based on the premise that immigrants should integrate into Australian society. Migrants will be given every opportunity, consistent with this premise, to preserve and disseminate their ethnic heritage.

Such provisions may be regarded as unexceptional at first sight, but need to be seen in relation to other parts of the Ministerial statement, which clearly indicate that the intake of migrants would be monitored to ensure that it "sustains cohesion and harmony in Australian society". Although the policies adhere to the letter of the Racial Discrimination Act passed in 1975 by not discriminating against migrants, their concealed intent seems clear — migrants will have to integrate, i.e. fit in and conform.

Revisionism and an attempt to stem the growing tide of ethnic consciousness and pressure towards multiculturalism may have played a part in the Liberal Government's delaying tactics, which ensured that the Report of the Committee on Teaching of Migrant Languages in Schools, set up in November 1974 by the Labor Government of the day, and presented in March 1976, was not tabled in Parliament until 8

December 1976. It was left in limbo for some six months before being debated and accepted. An alternative explanation for delaying the Report is the possibility that the Liberal Government did not want its findings and recommendations to prejudice the terms of reference of two committees it established in 1977. Both of them have played a major part in determining the direction of ethnic relations since that date.

The first, the Australian Ethnic Affairs Council, was set up on 31 January 1977 to advise the Minister for Immigration and Ethnic Affairs on a variety of issues relating to migrants in Australia. Most of the work is carried out through three sub-committees: Settlement Programs, Multicultural Education, Community Consultation and Ethnic Media. The Council's overall ideology was expressed by its chairman, Professor J. Zubrzycki (1977: 62), a sociologist of some eminence, but whose views are cast in the dated mould of Talcott Parsons' grand theory and holistic approach, and reflect his political conservatism and theoretically "safe" stance:

> "We are to serve Australia, the whole nation, all of us, whatever our native tongue. The task is stupendous for we must make up our minds, whether we are to look backwards on what used to be rightly called British civilization in Australia or, whether we are to have a future as a multi-lingual, multi-racial, multi-cultural Australia."

The Council published its response to the Australian Population and Immigration Council's Green Paper, *Immigration Policies and Australia's Population*, in August 1977 under the title, *Australia as a Multicultural Society* (AEAC, 1977), which gives a guide to the Council's ideological framework. It is fleshed out in the publication with detailed consideration of three concepts which constitute the cornerstone of its thinking then and subsequently. They are social cohesion, equality and cultural identity. Despite these ideas — which have assumed the force of condensation symbols, in other publications — the Council's views on schooling and curriculum for migrant children are almost entirely concerned with English language teaching (TESL), bilingual education, community language education and the support of ethnic schools, all very similar to the recommendations of the Labor

Government-initiated Committee on the Teaching of Migrant Languages in Schools. Nothing to rock the boat here.

The second committee to be set up in 1977 was the Review of Post-Arrival Programs and Services to Migrants, in September of that year "to examine and report on the effectiveness of the Commonwealth's programs and services for those who have migrated to Australia, including programs and services provided by non-government organizations which receive Commonwealth assistance, and shall identify any areas of need or duplication of programs or services" (Galbally, 1978: 1). The chairman of this Committee was Mr Frank Galbally, a Melbourne criminal defence lawyer. Apparently he was a confidant of the Liberal Prime Minister, Malcolm Fraser, and was later appointed to several influential positions related to multicultural and ethnic issues. The committee's report was completed by 30 May 1978 and accepted by the Government before being debated in Parliament, or subjected to wider scrutiny by the media, the academic world and interested public. Extreme haste was necessary so that the Committee's recommendations to spend $.05 million for community languages in 1979 could be included in the Schools Commission's financial estimates for education for that year, which had to reach Treasury by 31 July 1978, in order to get into the August Budget.

The Galbally Committee had recommended the establishment of a national committee of recognized experts in education and pluralism to look at the whole question of migrant education throughout Australia, and set what many would see as an unrealistic deadline of three months for the completion of its work and report. In the event, the Schools Commission pre-empted the whole matter and on 30 June 1978 set up what was essentially a small sub-committee largely from its own members, including one or two token ethnics, but including no recognized expert in pluralist education. The Committee's final report (Committee on Multicultural Education, 1979) was in fact presented to the Schools Commission on 5 January 1979, but its recommendations for the allocation of the $.05m budgeted for 1979 got to the Schools Commission before 31 July 1978. Not only did the January report bear obvious signs of a hastily prepared document in its tacit acceptance of the many fallacies in multicultural education, but was also locked into an approach to the teaching of community languages, on which the $.05m would be spent, that did not reflect its own thinking but that of the Galbally Committee. As the Committee on Multicultural Education (1979: 3–4) makes clear in its report:

> "The fact that the Government had decided that the funds to be made available in the first year of the three year program were to be used for the fostering of the teaching of community languages had a considerable influence on the work of the Committee and on the recommendations made in relation to 1980 and 1981."

In other words, educational decisions having considerable bearing on curriculum selection and organization were made for blatantly political reasons. In fact, the Galbally Committee itself and its report cannot be exempted from this criticism. Stockley (1978: 23) has suggested that the Prime Minister, Malcolm Fraser, had taken a personal interest in the ethnic question which was not unconnected with concern to woo the ethnic vote, and could well have appointed a compliant chairman, Mr Frank Galbally, who would ensure that the report would not be overly critical of Anglo-Celtic control over education and other major institutions.

This conclusion is prompted by the recommendations in the chapter of the report on education, which can be criticized on several grounds. The Committee adopted the dated Tylorean definition of culture and stressed its expressive aspects, such as traditions, heritage, community languages and customs relevant to immigrant lifestyles, thus setting multicultural education on a course which has little to do with the life chances of migrant children. Despite this, the clear implication of much of the chapter is that the kind of multicultural education being advocated will increase equality of opportunity for all children. Without citing evidence to support its claim, the Committee also advocated multicultural education as a way of reducing prejudice and discrimination between members of different ethnic groups. Minimal awareness of the mass of research on contact hypotheses might have made the committee extremely wary of such a recommendation, for which there is little hard supporting evidence. Instead it had recourse to what has become virtual folk wisdom in this area — that "understanding one another" breeds tolerance. The Committee is even less aware of research findings and the mass of contentious literature on the subject of racial differences to judge from its ridiculous, sweeping assertion that "the concept of race is clear" (Galbally, 1978: 104). Apart from this, race is ignored as an issue despite clear demographic and research evidence that racism is a growing problem in Australia. The whole emphasis is placed on culture, even to the extent of equating ethnicity solely with cultural differences.

From the theoretical viewpoint of this book it could well be held that the whole chapter on multicultural education was designed to maintain Anglo-Celtic domination over the curriculum and access to instrumental knowledge that would enhance the life chances of immigrant children. The whole report is of dubious efficacy, in fact. It claimed to provide an "integrated package of measures for introduction over a period of three years, to enable the Commonwealth government to take further steps to encourage multiculturalism . . . [having] regard to the limits of acceptable resources" (Galbally, 1978: 3, 6).

However, Michael Liffman (1979), a leading activist in migrant affairs, has criticized the report for being either naïve or cynical if viewed from the standpoint of migrants' interests, possibly because it rests on bureaucratic assumptions which do not match the reality of power disparities and levels of discrimination in Australia. For example, the report recommends ethnic radio and television on the assumption that they will reduce prejudice and discrimination. However, if these do not significantly reduce the socio-economic disadvantages in Australian society, whether real or perceived by migrants, then it is hard to see how the attitudes of prejudice and discrimination that disadvantage generates (Schermerhorn, 1970: 220) will be changed. In short, the report is naïve because it is insensitive to structural power disparities built into Australian society. For similar reasons the report can be interpreted as a cynical exercise, and a pretence of action. Like the Australian Ethnic Affairs Council's (1977) publication, *Australia as a Multicultural Society*, before it, great stress is laid on the claim that multicultural education and the whole multicultural approach will alleviate inequality and provide greater equality of opportunity for migrants. However, if the "limits of acceptable resources" are such as to curtail what can be done and the members of the Galbally Committee knew this, then it needs to be asked what underlying reasons or "hidden agenda" made them profess an ideology of equality of opportunity but not provide the resources to change the situation in reality. This is tantamount to obfuscating the central problem of socio-economic disadvantage in Australia by the rhetoric and myth that multiculturalism will change it. As Foster has commented in summary (Foster, 1981: 364):

> "The Galbally Report seems to imply that multiculturalism is not a fact with social consequences, but simply an attitude to be encouraged. Education is singled out in the report as the institution which can bring about such a change in attitude [an interesting parallel with developments in England in the 1980s — my interpolation] and counteract the established elements of *monocultural* Australian society. Questions that arise from this stance concerning education and social change are not confronted in the Report. There is no discussion of structural changes in society which must accompany an educational policy designed to influence attitudes."

This has been the focus of attacks by some academics on the Galbally Report and its successors from official bodies (e.g. Australian Population and Immigration Council and Australian Ethnic Affairs Council, 1979; Schools Commission, 1981; Australian Council on Population and Ethnic Affairs, 1982), in what can be termed the post-Galbally "pluralist debate" (Bullivant, 1982b). On one side of the debate considerable opposition to multiculturalism and a multicultural Australia has been expressed by writers such as Professor Chipman (1978) and Dr Frank Knopfelmacher (Warnecke, 1981) on the grounds that they are socially divisive and in the latter's opinion could lead to "the ghetto and the ethnic cauldron" due to the fragmentation of the political and cultural structure of Australia's predominantly Anglo-Celtic society. On the other extreme side the high priest of multiculturalism, Al Grassby, continues to support it unreservedly (Warnecke, 1981): "We are the most cosmopolitan nation on Earth. Why try to fight it? Why not grab it, and take advantage of it?" In the middle of the continuum a vigorous academic debate continues with George Smolicz of Adelaide University advocating a kind of "stable multiculturalism", one of three varieties he has devised in yet another typology of cultural pluralism (Smolicz, 1981). Such a mode of analysis is not without its drawbacks and devising typologies has been criticized cogently by Leach (1961: 2) as "typological butterfly collecting". Opposing this kind of thinking are my writings and those of others who demonstrate how the current debate dodges issues such as the structural determinants of the disadvantages members of ethnic groups still experience. Professor Zubrzycki appears to be becoming more cautious about giving multiculturalism the unqualified support he gave it in 1977. In 1979 (Zubrzycki, 1979) he was prepared to concede that there are limits to multiculturalism especially in the risk of ethnic separatism jeopardizing social cohesion. More recently, (Warnecke, 1981) he fears a community backlash if ethnic cultural identity is promoted at the expense of social cohesion. Indeed there is some evidence that the amount of Federal money being poured into proliferating ethnic schools is generating resentment among Anglo-Australians. Zubrzycki also acknowledges that equal access to social and economic resources for members of ethnic groups is lagging behind the planned implementation of multiculturalism.

Meanwhile, at the official bureaucratic level, there continues to be a flood of publications from the "ideological state apparatus", which have all the characteristics of a stage in the evolution of an ideology when it is reformulated and revised to meet counter-ideological criticism. In the most recent publication of the Australian Council on Population and Ethnic Affairs (1982), *Multiculturalism for All Australians. Our Developing Nationhood* (chaired by Professor Zubrzycki), the great trilogy of social cohesion, cultural identity, and equality of oportunity has been bolstered by a fourth, "equal responsibility for, commitment to and participation in society" (ACPEA, 1982: 12). This is accompanied by a number of question-begging assertions designed to head off the criticisms that might be levelled against this reformulation of the ideology.

However, the "educational ideals" this Council advocates, based on the report of the Australian Ethnic Affairs Council's Committee on Multicultural Education, *Perspectives on Multicultural Education* (AEAC, 1981), verge on the banal:

— intercultural understanding, tolerance of and respect
    for cultural patterns other than one's own;

— improved communication between members of one cultural group and those of others;

— maintaining and nurturing the cultural and linguistic heritages within society.

In short, what is advocated does not envisage anything other than a bland, safe panacea and certainly not something that might challenge the continued Anglo-Celtic dominance in much of the general curriculum in Australia. Even the Schools Commission, once renowned for its ideological pace-setting, appears to be having second thoughts in its latest *Report for the Triennium 1982–84* (Schools Commission, 1981). It clouds the issues involved by including some questionable components of pluralism (Schools Commission, 1981: 16):

"The intellectual content of all schooling should reflect plurality — class, race, ethnicity, gender and community are ever-present realities upon which teaching must draw . . . Students should also be aware of non-ethnic differences and be able to examine the attitudes and beliefs held by a variety of sub-cultures which comprise our society."

There is no doubt that various government bodies are well aware of structural issues and the risk of what might happen if ethnic groups set up their own institutions in an attempt to obtain a fairer share of the socio-economic rewards and resources in Australia. It is clear that such structural and institutional pluralism would not be tolerated. As the Australian Population and Immigration Council and Australian Ethnic Affairs Council (1979: 4) has stated:

"A major cause for concern is whether the creation of a network of ethnic organizations and the formalization of group differences will adversely affect national unity . . . This is a delicate subject, but also a crucial one. It would certainly be legitimate for Government in a multicultural society to prevent the formation of divisive institutions that threatened national security."

A basically similar warning was issued by the Australian Council on Population and Ethnic Affairs in 1982. However, the Council (1982: 30) went further and stressed the government's obligation to maintain control over *cultural* deviancy, i.e. a major strategy of hegemony:

> "Inevitably there will be clashes between the core culture and elements of the minority cultures making up our society . . . However, where clashes occur, the core culture must prevail until it is modified by consensus or by appropriate authoritative action. However, in some cases of conflict, such as over human rights and freedoms, society and governments should be insistent that the core culture [Anglo-Celtic? — my interpolation] prevail without modification. In such situations, the Council would envisage the rejection of the offending element of the inconsistent culture."

In other words structural pluralism that goes too far will not be tolerated, neither will too much cultural diversity if it stretches to cultural deviancy. Such an official policy is not only ideological and hegemonic, but could also be doomed to failure, if ethnic groups attempt to provide for their own needs.

For example, the ethnic school movement and structures grow apace in Australia and there are signs that ethnic groups, including Aborigines, may be seeking to establish other institutions and structures to represent their interests. In addition, an Australian National Opinion Poll was taken in August 1981, a time when Vietnamese and Indo-Chinese refugees were pouring into Australia and recession was gathering pace. It showed (ANOP, 1981) that there is some fear (and growing fear) of racial trouble, widespread resistance to Asian immigration, and a strong desire to keep Australia white. Forty-eight per cent of responses thought that too many Asians were being admitted, 49 per cent were willing to admit that Australia is a racist country. The greatest perceived disadvantage of Asian immigration was the fact that Asians take away jobs from Australians. Ironically, only 21 per cent of the population could give a reasonable estimate of the number of Asians living in Australia (2.4 per cent according to the latest Australian Bureau of Statistics estimates). All this gives a distinct sense of *déjà vu*, harking back to the White Australia Policy.

Marie de Lepervanche (1980: 25) has suggested that the historical evolution of ideologies of pluralism in Australia can be interpreted as "a series of ideological transformations in the recreation of hege-mony". The latest would appear to be multiculturalism. Whether it too will evolve into something else as racism increases and/or ethnic groups set up more structures remains to be seen. To judge from the rapid development of organizations designed to assist Aborigines that have occurred in the 1970s and more recently this is a distinct possibility. Reliance solely on a naïve form of cultural pluralism will not alleviate the discrimination these people and many members of other ethnic groups still experience. Structural and institutional pluralism must accompany it, but inevitably this will be resisted as much as possible by the dominant Anglo-Celtic majority. Minorities will then have to devise means of usurpation to enhance their own interests and also maintain an element of social closure or exclusion which attempts to protect them from majority dominance. In Chapter 4 the Aboriginal land rights issue and strategies of usurpation adopted by a number of Aboriginal groups are discussed to illustrate the kinds of development that might be needed to achieve more equitable distribution of socio-economic resources and better life chances among all ethnic groups.

Notes to Chapter 3

1. In part, this Chapter draws heavily upon and attempts to update material presented in my earlier work, *The Pluralist Dilemma in Education: Six Case Studies*.
2. Both bodies were disbanded in 1981 by the so-called "Razor Gang" of the Liberal Government, ostensibly for financial economy, although the move could equally be interpeted as a way of removing challenges and criticisms of Federal policy arising out of the research and development both bodies promoted.

4 Structural and cultural adaptation

Aboriginal land rights and political gains since the 1970s

The referendum held throughout Australia in 1967, which abolished Section 127 of the Federal Constitution and gave the Commonwealth Government power to legislate in respect of Aboriginal affairs, was probably a catalyst for the events that have occurred during the 1970s and early 1980s. Prior to 1967 the official ideology and policy towards Aborigines had been assimilationist, matching those adopted towards immigrants. After 1967 a gradual evolution of policy and ideology occurred, so that by the election of a Federal Labor Government under Gough Whitlam in 1972 "self-determination" became the official orthodoxy. It was accompanied by "clear statements supporting local autonomy and decision making, substantial increases in access by local communities to federal funding, an improved Aboriginal participation in advisory and decision-making structures, and greater awareness within the wider community of the presence, problems and demands of Aboriginal people" (McConnochie, 1981: 17). Although the new policy was often poorly formulated and inadequately implemented, it nevertheless heralded the demise of a whole era of assimilationist approaches. It was also very much part and parcel of the reformist philosophies of the Labor Party.

When this government was thrown out of office in 1975 and a new Liberal Government elected there was a further change in government thinking towards Aborigines. This was from self-determination to self-management in 1975 which is the current approach to Aboriginal affairs, and reflects the "small-l" liberal ideology of reduced government control popular in this period.

Legal and administrative developments

The gradual evolution of new ideologies and policies has been accompanied by the creation of an administrative and legal framework at the structural level of the political system. After the success of the referendum in 1967, the Commonwealth Government speedily moved to set up a Council and Office of Aboriginal Affairs. The first Minister of Aboriginal Affairs, Hon. W. C. Wentworth, was appointed, and commented enthusiastically upon the implications of the new legislation which the referendum enabled. In the place of paternalistic legislation, "there is now discriminatory legislation in favour of Aboriginals. They enjoy the same legal privileges as other Australians, but in addition they have legal privileges of their own" (Wentworth, 1971). In addition to these moves on the part of the Commonwealth, all the States with the exception of Tasmania have enacted legislation throughout the 1960s and 1970s. In 1962 the South Australia Government passed legislation which had an assimilationist approach, Western Australia followed in 1963 with its new Native Welfare Act. In 1964 the Northern Territory's Aboriginals Ordinance was repealed and a new Ordinance passed in 1964 which covered the welfare needs of the general population as well as the Aborigines. Queensland passed a new Aborigines and Torres Strait Islanders Act in 1965, but it had a number of discriminatory features and powers of direct control over Aborigines on reservations in particular, which make it and the State Government itself the most repressive of all the Australian States. In 1967 the Victorian Government passed the Aboriginal Affairs Act "for the purpose of promoting the social and economic advancement of Aborigines in Victoria" (Preamble to the Act). New South Wales followed in 1969 with its new Aborigines Act.

It should not be assumed from this "almost feverish haste" to enact legislation which would provide special welfare and encourage Aborigines to leave isolated reserves and join the general community, that there has been an invariably favourable improvement in the lot of many Aborigines. The whole Aboriginal issue in Australia has provoked bitter arguments, tensions within and between States and the Commonwealth, and even divisions within the Aboriginal world itself, largely on grounds that campaigns for justice were not radical enough; were too radical; that spokesmen for Aboriginality were not really representative of their assumed constituencies; that certain groups, such as Torres Strait Islanders, were not catered for under legislation designed for mainland conditions; and a hundred and one other issues.

Queensland is still very much a rogue State in Aboriginal affairs and its squabbles with the Commonwealth Government illustrate the level of intransigence which characterizes its treatment of Aborigines (see Gale & Brookman, 1975: 73–76, especially Documents 22, 23 a–c). As a result of criticisms by Aborigines and the Commonwealth Government in 1970, Queensland's existing legislation was repealed and a new Aborigines Act was passed in 1971. Despite retention of a number of features which are still discriminatory the Act is an improvement on its predecessor — a situation which is also due to subsequent amendments. It is still obvious over issues such as land rights that the Queensland Government still considers that it need not defer to Commonwealth wishes or legislation; this situation is paralleled to a large extent by relationships between Western Australia and the Commonwealth.

In addition to legislation concerning the general social welfare and legal electoral status of Aborigines, legislation to improve their rights to land was also passed in the 1960s and 1970s, partly because they were encouraged to "press for the acknowledgement of their rights as prior occupants of Australia and to demand compensation [which] brought them into strong conflict with pastoral and mining interests in particular" (Gale & Brookman, 1975: 63). Thus South Australia passed its Aboriginal Lands Trust by law in 1966. "This body, composed of persons of Aboriginal descent, is vested with the ownership and administration of Aboriginal reserves in South Australia, subject to the approval of the Aboriginal councils on the reserves" (Gale & Brookman, 1975: 64). Similar legislation was passed in 1970 by the State of Victoria. Western Australia and New South Wales have also set up Land Trusts.

During the 1960s and 1970s the Commonwealth Government had direct responsibility for administering the Northern Territory (it has since become self-governing, like other States), and its legislation for land rights has become something of a pace-setter by which the efforts of other States may be judged. To understand how this has evolved it is necessary to say something of the events which occurred in the Territory in the mid-1960s and subsequently.

The Land Rights Campaign

The Aboriginal land rights campaign effectively began in 1966 when 170 Aborigines of the Gurindji tribe walked off a pastoral station, called Wave Hill and owned by the major company Vesteys in the Northern Territory, and set up their camp nearby at Wattie Creek. Initially the walk-off was a protest at wages and conditions on Wave Hill station, but it developed into a land rights case and "an assertion of a moral right to land, based on traditional associations. In time, the Gurindji at Wattie Creek attempted — eventually with success — to persuade Lord Vestey to give up a large part of the lease so that they could resume ritual associations with the land and develop a cattle station" (Yarwood & Knowling, 1982: 272). It should be noted that the Aborigines were assisted by white advisers and lawyers, some of whom, it was rumoured, were experienced campaigners in American land rights litigation by the Navajo Indian tribes of Arizona. However, little success was achieved and appeals to the Commonwealth Government virtually fell on deaf ears and were not taken seriously (Coombs, 1978). The Government was a coalition of Liberal (Conservative) and Country Party members, the latter being represented in Cabinet by such hard-line ministers as Peter Nixon, Ian Sinclair and Ralph Hunt, all farmers, who acted as spokesmen for the pastoralists. "The admission of Gurindji rights at Wattie Creek, based on traditional but not legal claims, was seen by Country Party members as a dangerous precedent, threatening white land-holders throughout Australia wherever there were Aboriginal communities" (Yarwood & Knowling, 1982: 272). Consequently little was achieved, apart from publicity favourable to the Aboriginal cause, until a new Labor government came to power in 1972. Even then, the major cause of the new legislation it enacted was not the Wave Hill dispute but another more complex one, and actually the first legal battle over Aboriginal land rights.

This had its roots in the decision by the Liberal-Country Party Commonwealth Government of 1952 to open up Arnhem Land in the

Northern Territory for mining, despite the fact that earlier legislation in 1931, by a Northern Territory Ordinance, had created the Arnhem Land Reserve. Part of it consisted of the Gove Peninsula where, at Yirrkala, a Methodist Mission had been established. After July 1938, the Methodist Missionary Society held a 21-year lease. However, on 22 February 1968, under the terms of the Minerals (Acquisition) Ordinance of 1953, the Commonwealth Government promised to grant a special mining lease to the multinational company Nabalco for a period of 42 years to "mine for bauxite, establish a township, and for other associated purposes" (ibid., p. 269). An important point at issue was that the area to be mined was "right on the doorstep" of Yirrkala Methodist Mission, homeground of 760 Aborigines (Souter, 1972: 20).

The matter was taken to the N.T. Supreme Court in the case of *Milirrpum and others v Nabalco Pty Ltd and the Commonwealth of Australia*, with counsel for the plaintiffs being Mr A. E. Woodward, and the defendants being represented by the Commonwealth Attorney and Solicitor Generals and private counsel. Mr Justice Blackburn found against the Aborigines' claim in a lengthy judgement. In this he held that "The doctrine of communal native title . . . did not form . . . part of the law of any part of Australia". Also he considered that "Such a doctrine has no place in a settled colony except under express statutory provisions". However, the crux of the judgement lay in the opinion that despite the fact that Mr Justice Blackburn found the Aborigines' "spiritual relationship to the land to be 'well proved' in terms of sacred sites and fertility rites, he did not accept that a particular clan had been shown to have 'a significant *economic* relationship' with a particular portion of land" (Yarwood & Knowling, 1982: 269 citing extracts from 17 *FLR*, pp. 143, 270–71 — authors' emphasis added). In other words, economic considerations entirely appropriate to white interests and culture were allowed to prevail over the spirituality of Aboriginal feelings for, and consequent claims to, land discussed in the first chapter. It is also significant that the judgement may have erred in law, as the initial justification for the resumption of land from the Arnhem Land reserve set up in 1931 was that it was no longer needed by Aborigines. Souter (1972: 20) has pointed out that this was strictly not true as 760 Aborigines attached to the Mission were using it.

It is relevant to note that the climate of the times in the late 1960s and early 1970s enabled the Yirrkala dispute to become a major issue and ultimately lead to far-reaching changes in Federal law, while a basically similar dispute a decade earlier generated far less impact. This was the granting of mineral leases to Comalco Pty Ltd, another aluminium multinational, by the Queensland Government in 1958 following the discovery of rich bauxite deposits at Weipa on the west coast of Cape York. On this occasion three missions and groups of Aborigines were involved at Weipa, Mapoon and Aurukun. However, Comalco gave assurances to them on the protection of Aboriginal interests, and gave promises to employ Aborigines in the development of the mine and subsequent processing of bauxite. Both assurances and promises were quickly broken and by September 1967 only six per cent of the employees were Aborigines. They were also subjected to discrimination, and on occasions, physical ill-treatment when they got drunk at the company bar. To allow them to use it had necessitated a relaxation of Queensland's liquor laws relating to Aborigines, but they were still not allowed to drink after 7 p.m. and were excluded completely on Tuesday and Thursday nights. As Frank Stevens commented after visiting Weipa, whereas "drunken European employees have been led off to bed, Aborigines have been handcuffed around trees until they have sobered up . . . in temperatures which frequently reach 95 degrees" (Stevens, 1969: 21). Alcoholism has become a major problem in many Aboriginal settlements and remains an almost intractable result of Aborigines' contact with the West.

To return to the Yirrkala dispute. Despite the defeat of the Aborigines' case, the matter was not dropped as it was far from settled in the minds of Aborigines. They sent a further petition to the Prime Minister in the Gupapunyngu language on 6 May 1971 following the adverse court decision. As an example of the dual economic and spiritual concerns that are emerging in the minds of many Aborigines, it deserves citing at length (Gale & Brookman, 1975: 83–84):

> "The people of Yirrkala have asked us to speak to you on their behalf. They are deeply shocked at the result of the recent Court case. We cannot be satisfied with anything less than ownership of the land. The land and law, the sacred places, songs, dances and language were given to

our ancestors by spirits Djangkawu and Barama. We are worried that without the land future generations could not maintain our culture . . . We gave permission for one mining company but we did not give away the land . . . The place does not belong to white man. They only want it for the money they can make. They will destroy plants, animal life and the culture of the people.

The people of Yirrkala want:
1. Title to our land.
2. A direct share of all royalties paid by Nabalco.
3. Royalties from all other businesses on the Aboriginal Reserves.
4. No other industries to be started without consent of the Yirrkala Council.
5. Land to be included in our title after mining is finished."

The petition and growing concern over the Yirrkala dispute led the Liberal Party Prime Minister William McMahon to make a statement in the House of Representatives on 26 January 1972. He virtually rejected advice from the Council for Aboriginal Affairs on land rights by stating that the Commonwealth Government "believes that at the right time and with proper safeguards the development of mineral resources on [Aboriginal] lands can contribute to the economic advancement of Aborigines resident on them and accordingly is prepared to grant exploration licences and mining tenements on Reserves to companies which are prepared to conduct their enterprises in genuine collaboration with the resident Aboriginal Australians" (McMahon, 1972). This statement provoked considerable criticism within Australia and overseas, and led to an Aboriginal protest which took the form of an orange and tan tent "embassy" erected on the lawns in front of Parliament House in Canberra. It coincided with the visit of Asian delegates who were in Canberra for the meeting of the South-East Asia Treaty Organization, and heightened the effect of the embassy. After months of fruitless discussion between Aborigines and government representatives, the tent embassy was forcibly removed by police, accompanied by considerable violence, which was given wide home and international coverage by the media, further harming Australia's image overseas. As a result of these events Aboriginal rights became a major issue in the election campaign of December 1972, which led to the success of the Labor Party and the election of a new government led by Gough Whitlam.

One of its earliest moves (through the Council for Aboriginal Affairs) was to appoint Mr Justice Woodward (Counsel for the plaintiffs in the Gove dispute) as a Royal Commissioner to advise on Aboriginal land rights, with a view to deciding how to implement decisions already taken to grant land to Aborigines. Mr Woodward's main findings, which were accepted by all three political parties, were (Yarwood & Knowling, 1982: 275):

1. That title to Aboriginal reserves and other land in the Northern Territory should be held by incorporated Land Trusts acting for the traditional owners.

2. That while minerals should be the property of the Crown (as with other land-owners), the Aboriginal owners should have a right of veto over mining, subject to an over-riding power of government, acting in the national interest.

3. The creation of an Aboriginal Land Commission to investigate traditional claims.

4. The creation of an Aboriginal Land Fund, to enable the purchase of land, where groups had established the strength of traditional claims.

The Whitlam Government moved relatively quickly to introduce a bill to give legal effect to the Woodward recommendations, but was dismissed from office in November 1975, before it could be enacted. However, the following Liberal Government under Malcolm Fraser took up the matter in 1976 and passed the Aboriginal Land Rights (Northern Territory Act) which was quickly used by Aboriginal communities to claim title to reservation land. By 1980 some 98,000 square kilometres, or 7.3 per cent of Northern Territory land area had been granted to Aborigines.

One matter which the Whitlam Government was able to resolve satisfactorily was the long-standing Wave Hill dispute between Vesteys

and the Gurindji people. In August 1975 Gough Whitlam symbolized
the handing over of a lease of 3,238 square kilometres to them by
pouring a handful of earth into the hands of a tribal elder Vincent
Lingiari, with the words:

> "Vincent Lingiari, I solemnly hand to you these deeds as
> proof in Australian law that these lands belong to the
> Gurindji people and I put into your hands this piece of
> earth itself as a sign that we restore them to you and your
> children forever."

As Coombs (the architect of the ceremony) describes (Coombs, 1978:
182), in reply Lingiari said in English " 'We are all mates now' and
then spoke to his people in their native tongue."

The present structure and operation of the Commonwealth Aboriginal Land Rights Act can be summarized briefly. The Act is designed
to give Aborigines in the Northern Territory inalienable freehold title
to their reserve lands which have been set aside for decades for their
exclusive use. Aborigines are enabled to make claim on traditional
grounds to vacant Crown land. Claims have to be proved before a
judge of the Territory's Supreme Court. Implicit in the Act is the
recognition that Aborigines have both spiritual and economic interest
in the land, and because of the vital spiritual link believe that land
cannot be lost, given away, bought or sold, but fear that it will be
destroyed together with ancestral spirits, thus leading to the destruction of the Aborigines themselves.

A system of Land Councils acting as agents for groups who want
to use the land has been set up, together with Land Trusts which are
the title-holding bodies. Councils and Trusts are made up of traditional Aboriginal owners and local representative Aborigines chosen
by their communities. Through these bodies Aborigines are able to
decide for themselves what they want to do with their land, and
traditional owners are able to be consulted to ascertain their wishes.
The Act defines traditional owners as being a local descent group of
Aborigines who have common affiliation with a site on the land
which gives them a primary responsibility for it, and entitles them by
Aboriginal tradition to forage over it. The process of identifying
traditional land owners involves procedures adopted by Land Coun-

cils using anthropologists, linguists, site survey officers and local council field officers, who record descent group membership and genealogies, and put them into written form for submission to the Land Commissioner.

The importance of sacred sites has been given formal recognition in the Northern Territory Aboriginal Sacred Sites Protection Authority. This was established in 1980 under a complementary legislative arrangement between the Northern Territory Government and the Federal Government, deriving from the Aboriginal Land Rights Act of 1976. Its duties, among others, are to establish and maintain a register of sacred sites, to examine and evaluate all claims for sacred sites made by Aborigines, to record sacred sites, and to recommend to the Territory Administrator that sacred sites be declared and to protect such sites. The Authority consists of twelve members of whom no fewer than seven shall be Aborigines chosen by the Administrator from nominations from the Land Councils.

Another important part of the 1976 Aboriginal Land Rights Act was the Aboriginal Land Funds Commission. Until 1980, when it ceased to exist, the Commission was responsible for buying up properties on the open market all over Australia, not solely in the Northern Territory. Properties are then leased on a long-term basis to Aboriginal Land Trusts and Land Councils. The successor to the Commission is the Australian Aboriginal Development Commission, whose wider powers include the purchase of land as well as capital items, such as housing, that it is empowered to deal with.

The crux of the land rights issue in Queensland and Western Australia — both containing large numbers of Aborigines — is that neither State recognizes the jurisdiction of the Commonwealth in matters relating to land rights, and refuses to be governed by the spirit, if not the letter of the 1976 Act and legislation that has followed. It will be recalled that this was at the back of the Noonkanbah dispute described in my first chapter. In that the Western Australian Government overruled Aboriginal objections to the oil rig scheduled to drill near a sacred site on a pastoral lease property bought for the Yungngora community by the Aboriginal Land Fund Commission. In the Premier, Sir Charles Court's, view at the time (1980):

"However the Commonwealth may regard such properties today, the State Government and the Commonwealth were in agreement that they were taken up as pastoral properties with the specific aim of helping Aborigines to develop their management skills and to generate economic independence to some degree at least . . . They are essentially pastoral properties where the old are secure and the young are given the opportunity to train properly for the options that are open to them.

They should not be seen as a permanent retreat to the dreamtime . . .

They are not to be regarded as a special form of land ownership for those Aborigines who happen to live on them, and certainly not as a source of unearned mineral wealth which would put some Aborigines in a favoured position in relation to neighbours whose properties were not endowed with such minerals or others who establish themselves in towns and cities through the arduous process of working for a living.

And perhaps most of all, from the Aboriginal viewpoint, they must not be regarded as land being occupied by some kind of divine right because of an attachment to the land through sacred sites or vague traditional links."

However specious Court's argument is, it does highlight the crux of the Noonkanbah dispute. Further on in his article Court makes the claim that many Aborigines in the State have no attachment to land, traditional, spiritual or otherwise, and have not been through the Law. In his view Western Australian Aborigines are almost totally detribalized and have nothing like the uninterrupted occupation of land which still applies in many parts of the Territory. The implications of this will be taken up later.

In accord with its rogue image, Queensland has also defied Commonwealth rulings and appeals on land rights, often by quite dubious semi-legalistic measures, legitimated by the paternalistic ideology of protectionism and segregation that still holds in the State, and may be traced back to the 1897 Protection of Aborigines and Restriction of the Sale of Opium Act. An example of the Queensland Government's high-handed action occurred in 1978, when it moved to take over the administration of formerly Uniting Church-controlled reserves of Aurukun and Mornington Island. To accomplish this in the face of public outcry and the criticism of the Commonwealth Government, the State Government degazetted the reserves, effectively robbing the Aborigines of any tenure. Its thinking appears to have been influenced by the views of the government-appointed and virtually government-dominated Aboriginal and Islander Commission set up in 1977 to review existing Queensland legislation. In its report (AIC, 1978: 15) the Commission specifically rejected any notion of Aboriginal land rights. It also considered that the communities on the existing reserves would "become part of the normal social structure of the State when they are no longer required for special use". The Commission observed that it "expressly does not support separate development in areas dedicated in perpetuity only for Aboriginal and Torres Strait Islander people", and envisaged reserve communities becoming "conventional country towns or local authority areas". The Commission also envisaged long-term leases to householders as the only security of tenure. However, community councils would be required to advise the Department of Aboriginal and Islander Affairs on the suitability of the tenant. Public statements from the Aboriginal North Queensland Land Council and the findings of a survey by the Aboriginal and Island Legal Service, in conjunction with the Foundation for Aboriginal and Islander Action Research in 1977, showed that Aboriginal Reserve Residents in Queensland "want far greater security of land tenure than fifty year leases to the community or leases to householders" (Foley, 1981: 39).

In spite of the public outcry against the resumption of direct control over the Aurukun and Mornington Reserves, the Queensland Government passed the Local Government (Aboriginal Lands) Act of 1978. This made shires of former reserves, granting the former communities a 50 year lease with no stated option of renewal. Section 32 of the Act places severe limitations on the power of the shire council over the leased land. Section 31 provides that all mineral rights shall be reserved for the Crown, together with free right of access to the land

and all rights of way. At the time of this legislation the Commonwealth Government passed its Aboriginal and Torres Strait Islanders (Queensland Reserves and Communities Self-Management) Act of 1978 in an attempt to forestall the Queensland Government's action. This Act was never used to back a High Court challenge to Queensland, but seemed to be merely a political token response (Foley, 1981: 41).

A more cynical use of power by the Queensland Government has directly concerned the Commonwealth's Aboriginal Land Fund Commission (ALFC). In 1975–76 the ALFC negotiated the sale of Archer River Downs, a pastoral leasehold on the western part of Cape York Peninsula and paid a deposit on the purchase price. The property was intended for the Winchinam group of Aborigines who were, and still are, forced to live at Aurukun. They are also the traditional owners of the Archer River Downs property. However, the Queensland Minister for Lands refused to transfer the lease and on 12 November 1977 the 166,000 hectare area was gazetted as the Archer River Bend National Park, thus effectively alienating it from Commonwealth control and Aboriginal use.

In summary then, the whole issue of land rights is clouded by State versus Commonwealth rivalries and the obdurate refusal of Queensland and Western Australia to grant freehold title to Aboriginal reserves. Throughout all the legal battles and protest movements that have characterized the 1970s, it seems clear that big business capital interests overthrow Aboriginal interests when mineral or oil rights are at stake. Despite some softening of its repressive measures Queensland remains the major obstacle to true land rights justice for Aborigines.

To round off this discussion of the political context, mention should be made of areas where Aboriginal gains have been more positive, even though they do not concern land rights. The Commonwealth Council and Office of Aboriginal Affairs eventually became the Department of Aboriginal Affairs, which has progressively implemented a variety of programmes and direct funding for Aboriginal advancement in housing needs, medical services, training of health workers and a variety of initiatives in the field of education, employment and training. A major feature of the 1970s has been the emergence of structures to enable Aborigines to express their own needs at the Federal level. The National Aboriginal Congress (NAC) was set up in 1977 as a successor to the previous National Aboriginal Consultative Committee. The purpose of the Congress (Watts, 1981: 63):

". . . is to provide a forum in which Aboriginal views may be expressed at State and National level and in particular, to express Aboriginal views on the long term goals and objectives which the Government should pursue and the programs it should adopt in Aboriginal affairs, and on the need for new programs in Aboriginal affairs."

Despite the fact that, strictly, it has only advisory powers, the Congress has proved significant structurally in strengthening Aboriginal claims. The Aboriginal Development Commission, which has already been mentioned, has representatives on it from the NAC and, like it, represents Aboriginal views to the Government. The Commission has an all-Aboriginal membership. The Aboriginal voice is increasingly being heard through the Aboriginal Consultative Group to the Schools Commission and its successor, the National Aboriginal Education Committee (with a full-time chairman and eighteen part-time Aboriginal members), together with Consultative Groups in each State. In a wider field Aborigines have greater say *inter alia* in the Council and Committees of the Australian Institute of Aboriginal Studies and the Aboriginal Arts Board of the Australia Council.

Structural and cultural adaptation

In Chapter 1, the centrality of land and its ancestor spirit-sacred site associations in traditional Aboriginal culture were discussed. From what has been described in this chapter, it is obvious that land still plays a major part in the resurgence of Aboriginal advancement. It is clear that gains have been made as a result of legal and political concessions on the part of the Commonwealth and various State governments. The reasons for their hegemonic control over land are clearly economic, being concerned with mineral exploitation and pastoral leases, both involving the interests of large Western businesses and multinational companies. However, despite usurping significant gains on the land rights issue, many groups of Aborigines have yet to evolve cultural programmes which support the necessary degree of inclusion to resist further attrition by Western dominance and values.

Some groups have apparently succeeded in doing so, and six case study examples are provided in what follows to illustrate how they are adapting aspects of traditional Aboriginal culture to present-day survival needs. In some cases land is both a symbolic and an economic base for the cultural programmes that are evolving. In other cases, components of traditional Aboriginal culture unrelated to land are being selected. What is more apparent, however, is the development of structures and institutions that are either uniquely Aboriginal or represent an Aboriginal adaptation of similar Western institutions. The resultant cultural and structural synthesis, going by the term Aboriginality in recent literature, may be the key to further Aboriginal advancement, and may also carry a message for other racial and ethnic groups in pluralist society. My analysis draws heavily on the work of Keith McConnochie and other Australian theorists who have tackled this issue.

Case 1 — Economic base dominant

A case where Aborigines have secured a strong integral economic base, within the introduced economy, but at the cost of virtually abandoning their Aboriginal heritage is described by Peter Sutton (1981: 6–7), an anthropologist who has worked with Aborigines in many parts of Australia. He cites an Aboriginal family of part-Aboriginal people in Cape York Peninsula who have managed over the last 50 years or so to control vast pastoral properties and associated facilities such as stores and post offices. These constitute a secure, wealthy economic base which has gained them respect in an area noted for white racism, even to the extent that whites have married men and women from the family without public disgrace. However, although some of those who are middle-aged know some Aboriginal language, members of the family tend to publicly deny their Aboriginal origins, even to the extent of claiming that they are part-Maori. Sutton stresses that only the possession of a base in the local economy and playing active roles in it enables Aborigines to be taken seriously by whites, and to take themselves seriously as " 'people of substance', whether that involves control of money, of land, or of organizational structure of some scale" (ibid., p. 7). The role of land rights campaigns in this would appear to be crucial, as land provides the "economic and political capital" from which Aborigines can advance claims to justice. In this, the spiritual life and related traditional culture can even be considered of quite secondary importance (ibid., p. 6):

> "Historically, loss of land must be seen as having been more damaging than loss of distinctively Aboriginal cultural expression such as language or dances, or even loss of life through violence, when we are considering the long-term processes by which Aborigines have suffered. By effectively losing their land, many Aboriginal people have lost not just independently controlled living space but their foothold in economic life. From being integral participants in a hunter-gatherer economy, many have moved to being marginal to any economy."

This group survives through having a strong economic base.

Case 2 — Lockhart River — ideational base dominant

Lockhart River, described by Athol Chase, an anthropologist in the School of Australian Environmental Studies, Griffiths University, Brisbane (Chase, 1981: 23–27), is a small Aboriginal community of some 350 people in Cape York Peninsula originally formed in 1924 as an Anglican Mission station. In the 1960s the settlement was taken over by the Queensland Government's Department of Aboriginal and Islander Advancement. Due to intermarriage with Torres Strait Islanders, to European eyes the Lockhart River group do not look Aboriginal, and also appear to have "lost their culture". Europeans claim to see evidence for this in the fact that the Aboriginal language among the young has been replaced by creole, the Aborigines use no traditional weapons or other artefacts in hunting and gathering, and there is a relative absence of corroborees or ceremonial gatherings. In their place the Aborigines have adopted introduced Pacific, Torres Strait "island style" dances and songs. Additionally, Europeans note the fact that the Aborigines have "given up reliance on bush foods and hunting trips for the attractions of a beer canteen and store foods"

(Chase, 1981: 24). Europeans also believe that some vestiges of traditional Aboriginal culture still exist in the practice of hunting for
dugong and turtle, even though in dinghies equipped with outboard
engines, and the apparent inability of Aborigines to maintain expen-
sive machinery, hold their liquor, preserve European standards of
health and sanitation, and in their constant feuding. Many of the last
opinions verge on stereotyping, but the essential point about the
European view of Aboriginal culture is the emphasis placed on *visible*
technological aspects, relationships with the natural environment and
artefacts. There is little attempt to credit the Lockhart River people
with any *invisible* ideational base in terms of beliefs, ideas and values
different from those of Europeans.

In contrast, members of the group see themselves as heirs to and
descendants of pre-contact Aboriginal groups that have occupied their
part of the Cape York coast for centuries. They have a well-established
history "which accounts for their presence there as a distinct category
of human beings from the time of creation" (ibid., p. 25). Other
groups on the Peninsula recognize this continuity. The Lockhart people
simply "belong" to the bit of territory they inhabit, and this is undis-
puted. Older people can delineate all the clan territories and the many
sites they contain, together with the various correct behaviours that
belong there. There are connected beliefs about ties between particular
families and tracts of land, and also between certain people and the
resources these tracts contain. Such beliefs are based on complex ideas
about the classifications of people on the basis of kinship, marriage and
descent. Despite living in close proximity in European-style bunga-
lows, Lockhart River people still interact with each other following
rules based on these classifications. Strict rules operate in terms
of respecting personal space, addressing persons, distribution of
resources — whether they be food or European artefacts, and support during fights. Material technology and artefacts are far
subordinate to the intricacies of coping with the social and metaphysical environments. In this group traditional ideas from the
ideational and epistemological side of the cultural survival programme predominate.

Case 3 — "Mimili" (Everard Park) — neo-traditionalist culture dominant

"Mimili", as its inhabitants prefer to call it, is an Aboriginal community living on, and in tenuous association with, a cattle property (Everard Park) in arid north-west of South Australia.[1] The cattle station management calls on the Aborigines only for seasonal pastoral work, otherwise the community is free to follow traditional ways, provided they refrain from alcohol and camp away from the homestead. There is no school, no store, no hotel, no housing, no hospital. Apart from the receipt of regular social welfare benefits which make up part of their limited cash income contact with the State's departmental welfare services is minimal.

The population of the group consists of about 100 to 150 people of whom nearly 40 per cent are under ten years of age. They are highly mobile within a large but clearly defined area and at any one time many are likely to be away hunting, visiting relatives or friends on neighbouring missions or settlements, arranging ceremonies or engaging in seasonal work elsewhere. Hunting for native animals is still the most important way of obtaining food; white flour has become a substitute for seeds and other forage items destroyed by cattle, although wild figs are still gathered. The limited cash income is not usually spent on food, clothing or European goods, but goes mainly towards buying motor vehicles to assist traditional hunting, social and ritual activities and extend their range. Cash is also used to give gifts to relatives strictly in accordance with traditional obligations. As Coombs comments (cited in Gale & Brookman, 1975: 117):

> "Indeed life for the Mimili people still centres around their traditional social and ceremonial life. The people have links with communities to the north and west and, for men's and women's rituals, small groups travel between these centres planning, co-ordinating and carrying out ceremonies . . . The advent of the motor car has made all ceremonies easier to arrange and they have become more frequent in recent years. Perhaps this change has been encouraged by the fact that the old men who are the bearers of important ritual responsibilities, also possess in their pensions the financial means of access to vehicles. While

this pattern of expenditure, and the relative values it
reflects, persists, they probably will continue to be a relatively affluent community."

The Commonwealth Government has recently purchased the
pastoral property and handed it over to the group at an emotional and,
on the part of many Aborigines, tearful ceremony. It will be run as a
cattle station initially with the help of a white manager who must first
be "vetted" by the Aborigines. They seek to involve white residents
and long-term visitors in their own communal structure and establish
relationships with them that "reflect and are compatible with the
pattern of mutual obligations which underly that structure" (ibid.,
p. 119). What will happen when the Aborigines get caught up in all the
details of cattle-raising economy, involving massive changes in out-
look, is for the future. But as Coombs (ibid., pp. 119–20) points out:

"For the Mimili Aborigines, however, there seems to me
for the present little uncertainty about their vision of the
future desired and expected. It is essentially Aboriginal
and traditional — a grander and more vigorous version of
their immediate past — a life dedicated to the traditions
and ceremonies of their totemic ancestors — taking from
the white technology and white society, ruthlessly and
without question, only those things which serve its purpose, honouring the obligations its traditions impose but
recognizing none that are incompatible with it."

Whether such a neo-traditionalist culture will provide a survival base
remains to be seen.

*Case 4 — Strelley — European economic base and traditional synthesis:
controlled adaptation*

Strelley, described by McConnochie (1981) and Liberman (1981),
is a community of about 600 Aborigines speaking Nyangumarta,
Mantjiltjarra and Kukatja languages in the north west of Western
Australia. The community has a long history of determined independence dating back to the strike in the Pilbara region in 1946. The
community owns and operates a number of pastoral stations near Port

Hedland and has "achieved a unique level of economic and social independence" (McConnochie, 1981: 10). The community is also highly traditionally oriented and is "determined to maintain a modified but distinctive Aboriginal culture within the broader economic and political structures of Australian society".

The community opposed the location of a Government State school in its area on the grounds that it would threaten traditions and the survival of the group. In 1975, however, the community obtained enough funds to enable them to provide their own school which is based on traditional community structures, controlled by an all-Aboriginal council, and with classes conducted outside in the camps and under close observance by the local community. The curriculum includes some native language literacy classes and some numeracy. The latter focuses on Aboriginal activities like hunting or gathering pearls; the former mainly concentrates on elements of everyday Aboriginal life, using texts specially prepared at the settlement. European teachers are only concerned with teaching English and numeracy. Aboriginal elders or teachers are concerned with other aspects. "No instruction is given that would conflict with the traditions of the sacred Aboriginal Law, which is maintained throughout the activities at Strelley as the best guarantee of a strong Aboriginal culture" (Liberman, 1981: 141–142).

The key to Strelley's present culture is the economic base on which it depends. Unlike the previous case of a virtually uncompromising, ruthlessly exploitative community at Mimili, Strelley has adopted a modified version of Aboriginal culture as McConnochie (1981: 19–20) describes, through controlled adaptation:

> "The economic structures at Strelley . . . have been influential in modifying both the cultural outcomes and the epistemological base. The commitment to a group identity which extends beyond traditional kinship structures has led to the emergence of an economy within the community which allocates responsibilities and material benefits across the whole community, including the children, on a deliberate and equitable basis which, while modifying traditional structures, emphasizes the group interdependence. Strelley

operates within a centralized authority structure which, while not existing within the traditional Aboriginal structures, has been an essential component in the development of the Strelley community as a viable autonomous group. Authority structures, religious and aesthetic activities, economic activities, housing, health practices, and so on, have all been modified, to a greater or lesser degree, to be compatible with, and to support this economic structure."

On this basis, remarks McConnochie (1981: 21), Strelley is "furthest along the road to developing a sustainable, satisfying and identifiably Aboriginal culture". One can only speculate whether Mimili will have to adopt the same tactics of modification to survive, the more it gets involved in the cattle economy.

Case 5 — Yipirinya — fringe dwelling Aborigines

Another group discussed here, based on McConnochie (1981), is Yipirinya. This is a conglomerate, rather than a compact community, of some 1,500 Aboriginal people living in fringe camps around Alice Springs, in the Northern Territory. The groups involved have a historical and cultural background that varies considerably. Groups like the Aranda and Loritja have been living on the fringes of Alice Springs for several generations. Other groups, such as the Walbiri have come into the area only in the last five to ten years. It is necessary to distinguish the fringe dwellers from some 2,000 urban Aborigines in Alice Springs and from about 5,000 to 6,000 Aborigines living in settlements in the southern section of the Northern Territory.

The fringe dwellers share a number of what appear at first sight to be contradictory features. On the one hand they live in extreme poverty in humpy type camps of bashed tin, sacking and similar materials. They share a lack of sophistication in Western culture and lack of access to its major institutions. Unemployment is high, typically sporadic and, when obtained, usually in unskilled positions. There is a high level of dependence on white society, cash economy, social welfare benefits and handouts, but otherwise little involvement or influence in local, Territory or Federal politics.

On the other hand, the people of the Yipirinya fringe camps "live there by conscious choice. They realize that they must co-exist with the dominant non-Aboriginal society, but wish to retain their cultural identity within it. They are strong in their culture, speaking their own language and living in extended family groups according to the kinship system. They have retained their traditional orientation, sharing an Aboriginal world view based on the law, the land, and ceremonies. There are even numerous sacred sites around Alice Springs itself, some of which belonged to the Yipirinya dreaming" (McConnochie, 1981: 14–15). This quotation from the curriculum of the Yipirinya school seems unduly flattering as McConnochie's own analysis points to a situation where the "normative and aesthetic frameworks of the fringe dwelling camps are still in the process of development". There are tensions between the frameworks due to the peoples' involvement in and dependence on the Western economy and Alice Springs itself. The "pervasive presence of white culture, the alienation from land, the constant demands of white society for English language skills, and the continuous subjection to western legal demands . . . all demand a radically modified cultural system with a radically modified epistemological base" (ibid., p. 21). Constructing these will be "enormously complex, unpredictable and time consuming". However, it may be assisted partly by a community council, Tangentyera Council, a co-ordinating body established in the mid-1970s by the communities. It has been successful in "providing a focus of community identity, and in negotiating over obtaining special purpose leases for the communities, housing, and general improved health facilities" (ibid., p. 15). But from all reports the Alice Springs fringe dwellers have a long way to develop, before their levels of health, nutrition and general well-being in the material sense at least, ensure reasonable prospects of long-term survival.

Case 6 — Aborigines in urban settings — towards Aboriginality

The five examples which have been summarized above illustrate a variety of ways in which land plays a part in the cultural programmes — or lack of them — in the groups concerned, and do not exhaust all the features of this complex issue. To the increasing numbers of urban-dwelling Aborigines land rights are a "less particular and more emo-

tional issue" than they are to traditional elders trying to secure safeguards for their own particular territories and reserves (Gale &
Brookman, 1975: 110). However, even urban-based Aborigines are
not untouched in a practical way, as in 1975 the Commonwealth
Government allocated funds to purchase a block of inner suburban
land in Sydney which Aboriginal communities — now seen to be viable
— are developing as a housing and community area (ibid., p. 110).
The land rights question is used by the more outspoken Aboriginal
representatives and activists as a way of symbolizing their grievances
and politicizing the whole question of compensation and justice for
Aborigines. On the other hand, the respected Australian historian,
Professor Geoffrey Blainey, speaking on an Australian Broadcasting
Commission television programme in December 1982, was of the
opinion that giving Aborigines unlimited land would not lead to the
paradise they imagine, and could even lead to a reduced standard of
living for all.

The developing urban Aboriginal culture appears to be a very real
and possibly, in the long run, successful attempt to develop a survival
programme suitable for such an environment. The term "Aboriginality" is being used increasingly by Aborigines to refer to what is evolving. In Marcia Langton's view (1981: 16–22), that of an Aboriginal
activist, it would be erroneous to simply interpret the emerging cultural programme through conventional European frames of theory,
e.g. culture of poverty (Lewis, 1966; Valentine, 1969). "We have
rejected the notion that we are assimilating into the European population and adopting white lifestyles. We are exploring our own Aboriginality and are finding that the white social scientists cannot accept
our own view of ourselves . . . urban Aboriginal 'society' and 'culture'
must be seen as 'complete, integrated and consistent systems relevant
to their members — not merely as a truncated (or castrated) version of
any other socio-cultural system'."

Aspects of these systems that draw upon the traditional Aboriginal
culture can be briefly summarized. The family kinship system based on a
matrifocal family "as an accepted or perhaps even desired family form
for Aboriginal women and children arising out of particular social
conditions" (Langton, 1981: 18) is the basic domestic and affiliative
mode of organization. Aboriginal social and cultural values play a part

in contributing to it as a woman-focused family including mother, grand-
mothers, aunts and other female relatives provide a cultural core. They
remember and pass on to the children "the knowledge that provides
them with an identity in a crowded impersonal urban environment"
(ibid.). Barwick has described (Barwick: 1962) how urban Aborigines in
Victoria are maintaining kinship and regional affiliation for community
security that is both social and economic, and for the socialization of
children and maintenance of their identity. In such big cities as Melbourne
and Sydney — the latter in particular has a large Aboriginal population –
Aborigines have set up and run their own medical, legal and housing
organizations. Langton (ibid., p. 19) considers these to be a result of
movements in the 1960s which began to lift the stigma from Aborigines,
both in and out of cities, and give them the freedom to express their own
cultural aspirations in their own terms and idioms. Aborigines are even
using "white" organizations such as churches and unions for their own
ends in the process (ibid., p. 20). The stress on Aboriginality and
Aborigines using their own idioms is also acknowledged by Kolig (1977):

> "Aborigines . . . have to find identity in relation to 'the
> others' and this situation really is induced or enforced . . .
> they draw on *their* social intellect and the result ultimately is
> *their* Aboriginality, and not a by-product of white encroach-
> ment." [Author's emphasis]

In other words, Aboriginality is a form of subjective self-consciousness
and not an externally imposed objective attribute.

Aboriginality must be communicated through language, and here
too there may be developing an Aboriginal mode of communication
that is indigenous to the emerging urban Aboriginal culture. Research
by Diana Eades, a research student in linguistic anthropology at the
University of Queensland, suggests that a distinct form of "Aboriginal
Non-Standard English" appears to be developing. It often includes
Aboriginal words (i.e. diglossia), and has modified some grammar
rules. For example, there is no verb to be. An Aborigine says "I sick"
to mean "I am sick" (Eades, 1981: 13). Eades also stresses that this is a
concomitant of an emerging Aboriginal culture and not a debased
form of English. She also mentions the sharing of social security
benefits among members of an extended, matrifocal family in Brisbane

as an example of the way traditional Aboriginal values and rules of sharing food and hunted game have been adapted to suit urban living. Seen through European eyes, like the use of Aboriginal English, such a practice can be interpreted unfavourably. From the Aboriginal viewpoint, however, such sharing is a logical extension of long-held Aboriginal traditions.

Case studies compared

From what has been described it seems apparent that there are several cultural foci around which Aborigines are developing survival programmes to meet the needs of living with Western values and pressures. Land, whether as an economic base, or as a symbol for the politicization of grievances and demands, is one such focus. Deeply held traditional ideas and beliefs, i.e. an ideational base, is another. Both can be combined into a grid which is illustrated in the following diagram.

FIGURE 1   *An ideational/economic grid to analyse ethnic "survivability" and degree of group inclusion*

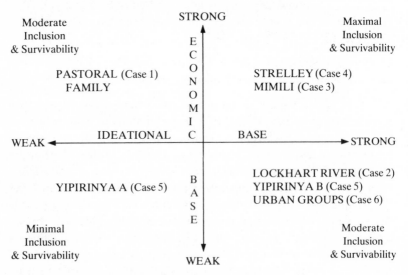

Note: Yipirinya A — External observer's assessment
Yipirinya B — Community members' assessment

Each of the six case studies can be located on the grid, to give some indication of the relative saliency of the economic base and ideational base, in providing Aborigines' "survivability" and capacity to maximize their advantage *as they perceive it*, and achieve a degree of inclusion. From the evidence available, the Strelley and Mimili communities seem to have developed a synthesis of both economic base and ideational base which maximizes survivability and inclusion. However, it should be noted that both groups have achieved this on their own quite differing terms. Strelley has opted for a modified version of the Western pastoral economy; Mimili has rejected it, apart from ruthless exploitation of social welfare payments and some wages. It also excludes whites (and is virtually excluded physically by them) unless they are willing to join the group, but strictly on its own, Aboriginal terms.

The pastoral family (Case 1) is obviously highly successful with a very strong economic base, but has virtually rejected the ideational component of Aboriginal culture. The Lockhart River group (Case 2) and the Urban Groups (Case 6) are economically weak but, if one accepts their own assertions, ideationally strong, though Urban Groups at least might appear to an external observer to be both spiritually and economically disadvantaged. Lack of clear evidence clouds the case of Yipirinya (A). From any external observer's point of view they must appear to be both ideationally and economically weak. Indeed, the Alice Springs fringe dwellers are generally regarded as one of the most deprived minorities in the whole of Australia. However, from the point of view of the group itself, as evidenced by the curriculum statement cited above, the community (Yipirinya B) regards itself as ideationally strong but economically weak.

If the pastoral family case is accepted as being of borderline validity, and if we recognize the limitations of this form of analysis, the grid does suggest the importance of the ideational base as a component in survivability, even though the economic base may be weak. It is completely erroneous and ethnocentric for whites to see Aborigines today as a dying "race" with a debased and decaying culture. Equally it would be foolish to ignore the appalling conditions under which many fringe and urban Aborigines live, termed by Kevin Gilbert, the Black activist (1977), a "human desolation". Coming through Marcia

Langton's and other Aboriginal writings is the conviction that even apparently "negative" aspects of current Aboriginal life should be interpreted as evolutionary steps towards a viable cultural resurgence. Whether this can be achieved without further development of Aboriginal structures that arouse defensive exclusion tactics from the Anglo-Celtic dominants remains to be seen. It may be that Aborigines are choosing what is virtually separate development, and it is worth recalling Professor Stanner's comment cited in Chapter 1 of this book (Stanner, 1979: 60–62): "The one thing that seems to continue is the effort of the restless, if baffled, Aborigines to work out terms of life they know how to handle . . . It is as plain as daylight that this system is still fundamentally Aboriginal in type". As will be apparent in the final chapter of this book, separatism and the evolution of an individual structural and cultural synthesis for every ethnic and racial group in a society can be regarded as the ultimate, extreme form of pluralism. It is one that obviously carries enormous dangers and some pluralist compromise must be achieved. This is one of the issues tackled in the chapter that follows.

Note to Chapter 4

1. "Mimili" is the ancient Aboriginal name of the homestead area. The "ethnographic present" is used in this account based on H. C. Coombs (1972).

5 Pluralism — pitfalls and potential

Towards a reassessment of cultural pluralism

The study of cultural pluralism poses numerous problems for the theorist, and the preceding chapters have attempted to present and illustrate some of the concepts and models that can be used to understand this complex phenomenon. In this chapter their implications are drawn together and rounded off.

Models of pluralism

Owing to the proliferation of theoretical writings in the whole area of pluralist relations, especially since the beginning of the twentieth century, models of pluralism have also tended to proliferate so that a bewildering range of choices confronts workers in the area. Many endeavour to develop their own models, often devising typologies of pluralist societies or types of pluralism. But this kind of exercise is pointless in the long run, as the lists that can be drawn up are virtually unlimited and can amount to little more than what Martindale (1961: 93) has termed "empty verbalisms". Alternatively one can use the models developed by leading theorists in this field. If one does, it must be remembered that their models were usually the product of a particular ideological stance — Marxism, colonialism, liberal democracy, for example — or were inspired by the particular and often unique pluralist features of the countries in which they did their research and developed their ideas. Models are also influenced by theoretical fashions in the social sciences which have come and gone over the years. All this does not mean that one should abandon the attempt to devise more powerful models and conceptual tools, merely that one should recognize that they too will be ideologically, historically and theoretically influenced.

The problem we are faced with is clear enough if one returns to first principles. Societies are aggregates of people usually inhabiting a certain delimited territorial space and arranging social relations between themselves so as to maximize their access collectively in groups or as individuals to whatever resources, rewards and satisfactions are available from the skills of others, the products of work and the materials available from the territorial space or environment. Society is much more complicated than this, of course, but the intention of using such a simple description is to emphasize that strictly this is all there is for the social scientist to work on — his primary social raw material, as it were. Using it in a process of conceptual mapping, model building and so on he attempts to delimit certain areas of the reality facing him, describe it, analyse it, and explain what is going on. But these are abstractions from reality and not reality itself, and are thus inherently limited.

Throughout this book the terms "plural society" and "cultural pluralism" have been used as if they are self-explanatory. Let us briefly look at some of their limitations and then attempt other formulations of social relations that may have higher explanatory power.

(a) Democratic pluralism — the pluralist society

Historically there have been two major traditions in theorizing about plural society — political and cultural. The first, democratic pluralism, is essentially a political theory, and originated in the nineteenth century, through such theorists as Alexis de Tocqueville. It attempts to describe and analyse the structure and operation of political systems with particular reference to the balance of power between competing religious, ethnic and economic groups, within a common set of political beliefs and values. A modern counterpart is Professor Cynthia Enloe, a North American theorist, whose views on the division of power provide one component in the type of model developed later in this chapter. She has pointed out (Enloe, 1981: 123–4): "The *state* is a vertical structure of public authority. It contrasts with the *nation*, which is essentially a horizontal network of trust and identity." The two concepts are frequently combined in the term "nation-state". The main features by which the state component can be identified are those structures and institutions that control "vertical authority". These are the civil bureaucracy, the military and police, and the judicial system. These "are rooted in, and dependent upon, horizontal bonds of trust and identification" (ibid.) among the groups and individuals that come under the jurisdiction of the nation-state as a whole.

Nation-states like Australia, Britain, the United States, Canada, New Zealand — to name only a few — have semi-planned economies over which the state component necessarily exerts considerable control. Institutions associated with the market system and the allocation of scarce resources and rewards come under the partial influence of the state, and one pluralist dilemma over which debate has raged since Plato has been over how much autonomy or power should be granted to citizens individually or in groups to pursue their own interests and how much should be the state's. Solutions range from totalitarianism (total state control) on the one hand to laissez-faire capitalism on the other.

Another way to conceptualize the nature of pluralism (e.g. Furnivall, 1948; Smith, 1965) draws on economic features of the nation-state as exemplified by colonial systems such as the West Indies and Netherlands India. In the latter (Furnivall, 1948: 304), the various ethnic and racial groups:

> ". . . mix but do not combine. Each group holds by its own religion, its own culture and language, its own ideas and ways. As individuals they meet, but only in the market place, in buying and selling. There is a plural society with different sections of the community living side by side, but separately, within the same political unit."

The point to note here is the implication that only one system of *political* control existed, that of the colonial power concerned, with the market economy being the "highest common factor" between the various sections (ibid., p. 310). In contrast, group relations in Western societies are not confined to the market place.

The issue of citizen autonomy versus state control extends to many other areas of social life. In education — another kind of "good" — for instance, Freeman Butts (1977: 6) has posed the issue in the United States in terms of two approaches to the "moral authority of public education". The first approach, "pluralism", maintains that the responsibility for education should be in the care of pluralistic communities and groups in a society. The second approach, "civism", maintains that authority should be under the control of the political or civic community. This inevitably implies considerable state control.

The ramifications of this apparently simple distinction are far-reaching. It will be recalled that one of the ways hegemony can be controlled by the dominant group in society is through depriving subordinate groups of the kind of knowledge and education that would enhance their life chances — a form of exclusion strategy. Where members of the various organizations and apparatuses that comprise the state are recruited from the dominant group, and there is a state-controlled education system, considerable opportunity exists for hegemony to be exerted through the curriculum and schooling. "Civism" versus "pluralism" can thus become a highly contentious issue, as witness the debate currently in Australia over the amount of Federal Government aid to be given to ethnic schools rather than to improving the provisions for ethnic children available in the state government school systems (Bullivant, 1982a; Lewins, 1980; Kringas & Lewins, 1981).

This tendency for knowledge to be differentially allocated according to the status of certain groups relative to the dominant group is not confined to capitalist or semi-planned societies such as America or Australia. It could well be a universal phenomenon in the opinion of Halsey *et al* (1980: 217):

> "The evidence from capitalist and communist countries alike is overwhelmingly that stratification along class, ethnic, status, or cultural lines heavily conditions both what knowledge is regarded as socially valuable and the eagerness and capacity of the children of the different strata to receive it."

In the above there is the question-begging assumption that societies are stratified — a familiar sociological, structural-functional model — but despite this reservation the message is clear. Knowledge and therefore access to educational routes to good employment, life chances and ultimately a share of resources and other rewards depends on one's membership of groups (strata in the structural model) that are marked by various attributes, i.e. class, status, culture, ethnicity and, it might have been added, race or phenotypical characteristics. Like the vertical authority of the state itself these can be ranked "vertically" — another common structural convention — rather than "horizontally", thus strengthening the impression that access to power is through channels appropriate to the state rather than through the nation.

A corollary of the state component is that it has only one set of structures or organizations controlling important social institutions such as the military and defence, law, education, the civil bureaucracy, economic market and currency system, social welfare system and others in the *public domain* of life, i.e. that shared by all members in the society. Even the language spoken by them is a public domain concern, especially if it is the only one employed in state-controlled or state-sanctioned media. What is meant by *structural pluralism* for the purposes of this book, *pace* Milton Gordon (1964) and referred to in previous chapters, is a form of society where there are separate sets of structures for major institutions, each set being maintained and controlled by distinct groups within the society. For example, there might be three or four legal systems, three or four languages, three or four political systems and their bureaucracies, three or four separate public education systems. There is no society on earth where this type of pluralism is found in such an extreme form, though South Africa, Switzerland and even possibly Canada with its francophone/anglophone division, exhibit some features that may be termed structurally pluralist.

Retaining the model for the moment, however, we can hypothesize further that each of the structure-maintaining groups could differentiate itself or be differentiated on a number of grounds — race (phenotypical differences), language and culture, ethnic affiliation, even possibly class. There is no logical reason why gender could not be such a boundary marker for inclusion and exclusion. Feminist groups have already demonstrated that it is possible to set up structures serving only women's interests and needs, though these still do not approach the degree of institutional structuring implied by the kind of structural pluralism meant here. Australian Aborigines described in cases above demonstrate that developing institutional structures is quite possible even though it can inevitably lead to separation from the wider society. The danger of full structural pluralism should be self-obvious. It is inherently a very competitive, conflict-prone situation in which separate groups compete for the resources and power available in the system of which they are a part.

(b) Cultural pluralism — the multicultural society

People who take part in structures occupy statuses and act out the behaviours or perform the roles associated with them. In essence, structures are also action systems. The structural status arrangements themselves, the rules governing role behaviours, and the selection of personnel thought fit to occupy the statuses all entail a considerable amount of knowledge and number of beliefs. These are available from the society's stock of public knowledge, i.e. its culture as defined in Chapter 1. Such knowledge "programmes' the structures and institutions of a society to function in one way and not others. Institutional structures and their cultural programmes are two sides of the same coin. Structural pluralism must inevitably entail cultural pluralism *and vice versa*. A fully culturally pluralist society, if the term is used in the accurate anthropological sense well argued by Despres (1968) must also be a structurally pluralist society.

Proponents of cultural pluralism (the second of the models) do not mean this, of course, and the father of the term, Horace Kallen (1956), made it very clear that a culturally pluralist society should not entail separate mini-states or political systems such as those entailed in structural pluralism. This makes nonsense of the claims one frequently finds in the literature, especially by the more romantic advocates of multiculturalism, that a multicultural society is made up of a number of separate "cultural groups", or "groups existing side by side and having different cultures", or worse, "cultures living side by side" without concomitant structures. Social groups, institutional structures and cultural programmes coexist: each cannot exist separately in any real sense without the others.

A further implication of the naïve or romantic use of the term cultural pluralism or multiculturalism is that members of cultural groups use their cultures in all aspects of their daily lives. But unless the society in which they live is also structurally pluralist, it is obvious that people move in and out of so many statuses and roles daily and adopt their related cultural programmes, that having to use one body of cultural knowledge would be extremely restricting.

This problem cannot be escaped by using the concept of multi- or poly-ethnic society, i.e. one in which there are a number of discreet ethnic groups. Each may have "a cultural focus on one or more symbolic elements" as Schermerhorn (1970: 12, cited above) points out, but these and even complete cultures will be singularly irrelevant when ethnics need to interact with the state's vertical systems and structures of power and control. As Despres (1975: 193) comments, "ethnic identities are rarely inclusive of the full range of social identities structured into poly-ethnic societies . . . individuals need not play ethnic roles all the time in order that poly-ethnic systems persist".

In what sense is cultural pluralism a valid, if still limited, concept? If the model proposed by Enloe is adopted, it seems feasible to suggest that the concept really only applies to the *horizontal* component of the nation-state, and not the vertical component. Ethnic loyalties and cultures can exist and complement or even challenge the feelings of trust and identity that are part of the nation. Provided challenge does not go too far, the state will be secure despite cultural diversity.

But the hard logic of ethnics' situation vis-à-vis the vertical component of the state remains. Here the dominant people of the state, the *Staatsvolk*, control a major part of the society's power and resources. For the nation-state to function as a viable entity this situation is desirable and inevitable. In Freeman Butts's terms cited above, civism must prevail over pluralism. A corollary is that the state must have an integrated culture and structure; full cultural and structural pluralism spells disaster. This need not apply to the horizontal component of the nation-state where cultural pluralism can exist as heterogeneity mainly in the sense of *cultural diversity* in the private domain of family, neighbourhood, local association and community, together with their respective structures and organizations. This is the kind of society that Despres (1968) maintains should strictly be termed only heterogeneous. Anything that really approaches structural and cultural pluralism threatens the cohesion of society.

The problem is to accommodate two views of society. On the one hand, the theory of democratic pluralism is mainly concerned with the issue of reconciling the competition that occurs between pluralist groups in a society with the need to preserve cohesion in the nation-state as a whole. On the other hand, cultural pluralism tries to explain how ethno-cultural and racial groups are able to maintain and gain respect for their heritages and identities, in the face of often hostile pressure from the majority group to assimilate. One solution, "dynamic pluralism", has been proposed by the theoriest, Richard Pratte (1979: 147–156). To him, individuals are born into, and owe primary allegiance to, their ethno-cultural groups. However, they are expected to move outside them into other special interest groups, when required to participate in political processes of the wider society.

Can the problem of integration and diversity be reconciled in any other way? The American theorist John Higham has addressed this issue and come up with the concept of *pluralistic integration* (Higham, 1975: 242–43):

> "In contrast to the integrationist model, it will not eliminate ethnic boundaries. But neither will it maintain them intact. It will uphold the validity of a common culture, to which all individuals have access [the culture of the state — my interpolation], while sustaining the efforts of minorities to preserve and enhance their own integrity. In principle this dual commitment can be met by distinguishing between boundaries and nucleus. No ethnic group under these terms may have the support of the general community in strengthening its boundaries. All boundaries are under-

stood to be permeable. Ethnic nuclei, on the other hand, are respected as enduring centers of social action."

Higham's formulation touches only on culture and not power: it is this issue which confounds attempts to come up with a fully satisfactory model of cultural pluralism and makes it desirable to hypothesize an alternative. In particular there is some danger that stratification analysis implies a greater degree of permanency and monolithic structure to groups than is actually the case. This is evident in analyzing monocultural societies where social class is conventionally the major means of differentiating groups for purposes of resource allocation. Stratification analogies risk being carried over simplistically into thinking about multi-ascriptive or pluralist societies where other diacritica are used.

To avoid monolithic structural models it seems preferable to conceptualize a pluralist society along lines foreshadowed in Chapter 2 of this book and similar to those implied by Banton's discussion of rational choice theory (Banton, 1983: 100–39). A pluralist society comprises individuals who act usually collectively but periodically in groups and associations to maximize their perceived economic and other advantages in institutional structures over other groups and associations. These are differentiated by using such boundary markers as class or status affiliation, phenotypical features, cultural lifestyle, language or dialect, ethnic affiliation, and other diacritica that may evolve through time, singly or in combination, to exclude those considered ineligible for group or associative rewards, and to include those considered eligible. The mere presence in a society of individuals or groups of different "races", ethnic affiliation, social class, etc. does not constitute pluralism if such diacritica are ignored or irrelevant in the processes of maximizing advantage.

Power and control

Such a formulation attempts to conceptualize a syncretic form of pluralism in a much less rigid way than is implied by models that use concepts such as strata or classes. Groups and associations vary in size, permanency and degree of structure and organization. Some form and dissolve irregularly as they are required, others such as the civil bureaucracy, legal machinery and other organizations of state control are obviously much larger and more permanent, but still not fixed in a monolithic group. Even in government, factions and coalitions are formed to pursue vested interests. Once these are achieved the associations are dissolved.

This in turn implies that the nature of power and control or hegemony even by government bodies may not be as monolithic, purposeful or indeed deliberate, as discussion in previous chapters may have suggested. Maximization of advantage through processes of inclusion and exclusion frequently may be far less rational than implied by the concept of rational choice theory, as Banton (1983: 108) points out. Similarly, the evolution of legitimating ideologies may reflect a much less calculating approach by those in power, and may instead be responses to outside pressures, panic reaction, whim, academic or other fashion, which are basically unrelated to any hegemonic intention.

The evolution of ideologies of pluralism in Australia discussed in Chapters 2 and 3 can be interpreted, probably accurately, as successive stages in the purposeful recreation of hegemony at least until the 1960s. The interests of "white" Anglo-Celtic groups and associations were promoted by using "race" as an exclusive boundary marker and Anglo-conformism as a strategy of inclusion. Hegemony was legitimated by the assimilationist ideology.

In the mid-1960s and thereafter, however, such an interpretation is less credible. The short adoption of the integration ideology may have been a stop-gap panic reaction to growing numbers of immigrants, and in Smolicz's (1971) opinion did not reflect any real change from the assimilation ideology. Grassby's adoption of multiculturalism in 1973 was as much copying an ideology then fashionable in Canada and America, with which he had contacts, as a result of deliberate hegemonic intent. Here, the ideology may have actually precipitated the changes that were ultimately labelled multiculturalism. In 1977 Grassby began to bracket "polyethnic" with multicultural in referring to Australia, but this was definitely taking over a term which had come into academic debate only that year but as a counter-ideology at the suggestion of this writer (Bullivant, 1977). Publications of the Australian Ethnic Affairs Council and related bodies appear to be casting around somewhat desperately for ways to reformulate and bolster a flagging ideology.

The Australian Schools Commission (1981: 112) appears to be both defensive and apologetic in defending multicuturalism, to judge from the following:

> "The desire of some people to define multiculturalism in a particular sociological sense rather than to use it simply as a term descriptive of the Australian situation, has led to claims that multiculturalism can be merely a slogan.
>
> The people who use multiculturalism primarily in a descriptive way do not see that it carries any particular connotation, certainly not the expectation that the nation will become one big happy family. Broadly, the term merely connotes differences of ethnic origin, race, religion and socio-economic class among the people of Australia. Narrowly used, it often refers to the presence of ethnic communities within the population. The specifics of what is needed to achieve equal opportunity for all of those people have yet to be worked out, but most groups realize that this will not be achieved without political action and struggle."

In the light of the previous theoretical discussion in this chapter the naïvety and simplistic thinking in this conceptualization of Australian pluralism should be self-evident. It is a far cry from the grandiose claims of the Galbally Report and Australian Ethnic Affairs Council described in Chapter 3 that multicultural education can achieve equality of opportunity and a more equal distribution of advantages regardless of race, ethnicity and the other boundary markers that are used as exclusive or inclusive strategies. The experience of Australian Aborigines described in Chapter 4 amply demonstrates the truth of the Schools Commission's warning that advantages and better life chances "will not be achieved without political action and struggle". Here at least the Schools Commission is being refreshingly honest, but the warning takes the matter of educating children from minority groups out of the horizontal dimension of the nation, where multicultural education is appropriate, into the vertical dimension of state and economic power, where it can never be applicable, as long as structural dimensions are ignored.

Other education systems such as those in Britain might take note of this problem before leaping so blithely onto the multicultural band-waggon, as appears to be occurring. By uncritically succumbing to "moral panic" produced by crises such as the Bristol, Liverpool or Brixton "race riots" of 1980–81 — a social "time bomb" known about but disregarded by all except earlier reports from committees of inquiry — the British education system may well have adopted an ideology it may yet come to regret. Its adoption may maximize one advantage for those in control of education, namely, a reduction of guilt, but it does not escape the obvious charge that educational solutions by themselves cannot bring about changes in the structure and strategies of social closure in society that result in massive inequalities and discrimination for those excluded on grounds of race, ethnicity and social class.

In effect, education systems in Britain, and possibly the Western world generally, could well be controlled unwittingly by a kind of educational hegemony legitimated by a meta-ideology and reconstruc-tionist philosophy of some antiquity, dating back at least to Rousseau. This is a firm belief in a form of social and liberal democracy in which solutions to political and economic problems are assumed to be cap-able of solution by educational means. As Green (1982) suggests, multicultural education may be the latest in a long tradition of social democratic education that has seen other fashions come and go. It is to be hoped that what has been proposed in this book about the real nature of power and control in pluralist societies may make some people pause and look again at the problems they pose.

Bibliography

ABORIGINAL ISLANDER COMMISSION 1978, Report to the Hon. the Minister for Aboriginal and Islander Affairs, 9 November. Brisbane.

ABORIGINAL RESEARCH CENTRE 1982, *Noonkanbah, August 1980.* Collected Documents. Melbourne: Aboriginal Research Centre, Monash University (mimeo).

ABORIGINAL WELFARE BOARD (NSW) 1953, *Circular.* Sydney: AWB.

ALTHUSSER, L. 1971, "Ideology and Ideological State Apparatuses". In L. ALTHUSSER, *Lenin and Philosophy and Other Essays.* London: New Left Books.

APPLE, M. W. 1979, *Ideology and Curriculum.* London: Routledge & Kegan Paul.

AUSTRALIAN COUNCIL ON POPULATION AND ETHNIC AFFAIRS 1982, *Multiculturalism for all Australians. Our developing nationhood.* Canberra: Australian Government Publishing Service.

AUSTRALIAN DEPARTMENT OF EDUCATION 1975, *Report of the Inquiry into Schools of High Migrant Density.* Canberra: Department of Education.

AUSTRALIAN ETHNIC AFFAIRS COUNCIL 1977, *Australia as a Multicultural Society.* Submission to the Australian Population and Immigration Council on the Green Paper, *Immigration Policies and Australia's Population.* Canberra: Australian Government Publishing Service.

AUSTRALIAN ETHNIC AFFAIRS COUNCIL COMMITTEE ON MULTICULTURAL EDUCATION 1981, *Perspectives on Multicultural Education.* Canberra: Australian Government Publishing Service.

AUSTRALIAN INFORMATION SERVICE 1976, *The Australian Aboriginals.* Canberra: AIS.

AUSTRALIAN INSTITUTE OF MULTICULTURAL AFFAIRS 1980, *Review of Multicultural and Migrant Education.* Melbourne: AIMA.

AUSTRALIAN NATIONAL OPINION POLL 1981, "Australia and Race". *The National Times*, 13–19 September, 28–29.

AUSTRALIAN POPULATION AND IMMIGRATION COUNCIL AND AUSTRALIAN
ETHNIC AFFAIRS COUNCIL 1979, *Multiculturalism and its Implications for
Immigration Policy*. Canberra: Australian Government Publishing Service.

BANTON, M. 1983, *Racial and ethnic competition*. Cambridge: Cambridge
University Press.

BARTH, F. (ed.) 1969, *Ethnic Groups and Boundaries*. Boston: Little, Brown.

BARTHES, R. 1973, *Mythologies*. Selected and translated from the French by
Annette Lavers. St Albans, Herts: Paladin.

BARWICK, D. 1962, "Economic absorption without assimilation? The case of
some Melbourne part-Aboriginal families". *Oceania*, 33(1), 18–23.

BENNETT, D. M. 1968, "The Study of Society in Australian Secondary
Schools". *Quarterly Review of Australian Education* 2(1).

BERGER, P. L., & LUCKMANN, T. 1971, *The Social Construction of Reality*.
Harmondsworth: Penguin University Books.

BERNDT, R. M., & BERNDT, C. H. 1964, *The World of the First Australians*.
Sydney: Ure Smith.

BERNDT, R. M., & PHILLIPS, E. S. 1973, *The Australian Aboriginal Heritage.
An Introduction through the Arts*. Sydney: Ure Smith.

BERNSTEIN, B. 1971, "On the classification and framing of educational knowledge". pp. 47–69 in M. F. D. YOUNG (ed.), *Knowledge and Control. New
Directions for the Sociology of Education*. London: Collier-Macmillan.

BIDNEY, D. 1967, *Theoretical Anthropology*. Second Edition. New York:
Schocken Press.

BLACKBURN, Mr Justice 1971, "Milirrpum v. Nabalco and the Commonwealth
of Australia". 17, *FLR*, 270–71.

BOCK, P. K. 1969, *Modern Cultural Anthropology: An Introduction*. New
York: Knopf.

BOSTOCK, W. W. (for Organizing Committee) 1977, Proceedings of the Conference *Towards a Multicultural Tasmania*. 25 June, Hobart: Multicultural
Conference Committee, University of Tasmania.

BOURDIEU, P. 1973, "Cultural Reproduction and Social Reproduction". In
R. BROWN (ed.), *Knowledge, Education, and Cultural Change*. London:
Tavistock.

BOURDIEU, P., & PASSERON, J-C. 1977, *Reproduction: In Education, Society
and Culture*. London: Sage.

BULLIVANT, B. M. 1972, "The Cultural Reality of Curriculum Development".
Education News, 13(9), 14–16.

— 1973a, "Is there a hidden curriculum in curriculum development?" *Twentieth
Century*, 27(3), 239–253.

— 1973b, *Educating the Immigrant Child: Concepts and Cases*. Sydney: Angus
and Robertson.

— 1975a, "Challenging conventional wisdom about educational processes in a multicultural region". *Papua New Guinea Journal of Education*, 11(2), 44–55, 68–74.

— 1975b, "Learning cultural realities through intercultural education: some dilemmas and solutions". In D. DUFTY & D. HARRIS (eds), *Learning About One Another*. Canberra: UNESCO.

— 1976, "Social control and migrant education". *The Australian and New Zealand Journal of Sociology*, 12(3), 174–183.

— 1977, "A Polyethnic Perspective on Teacher Education for International Understanding". 21–6 in G. COFFEY (ed.), *Teacher Education for International Understanding*. Canberra: Curriculum Development Centre.

— 1979, *Pluralism, Teacher Education, and Ideology*. The Report of the Survey of Teacher Education for Pluralist Societies, Parts 1 & 2. Melbourne: Monash University, Centre for Migrant Studies and Faculty of Education for ERDC.

— 1981a, *The Pluralist Dilemma in Education: Six Case Studies*. Sydney: George Allen & Unwin.

— 1981b, *Race, Ethnicity and Curriculum*. Melbourne: Macmillan.

— 1982a, "Power and control in the multi-ethnic school: towards a conceptual model". *Ethnic and Racial Studies*, 5(1), 53–70.

— 1982b, "Pluralist debate and educational policy — Australian style". *Journal of Multilingual and Multicultural Development*, 3(2), 129–147.

BUTTS, R. FREEMAN 1977, "The public school as moral authority". In R. F. BUTTS, D. H. PECKENPAUGH and H. KIRSCHENBAUM, *The School's Role as Moral Authority*. Washington, DC: Association for Supervision and Curriculum Development.

CHASE, A. 1981, "Empty vessels and loud noises. Views about aboriginality today". *Social Alternatives*, 2(2), August, 23–27.

CHIPMAN, L. 1978, "Multicultural myth". *Quadrant*, 22(3), 50–55.

COHEN, A. 1974, *Two dimensional Man*. London: Routledge & Kegan Paul.

COHEN, Y. A. 1971, "The shaping of men's minds: adaptations to the imperatives of culture". pp. 19–50 in M. L. WAX, S. DIAMOND & F. O. GEARING (eds), *Anthropological Perspectives on Education*. New York: Basic Books.

COMMITTEE ON MULTICULTURAL EDUCATION 1979, *Education for a Multicultural Society*. Report to the Schools Commission. Canberra: Schools Commission.

COMMONWEALTH DEPARTMENT OF IMMIGRATION 1963, *Digest*. Report of the Australian Citizenship Convention. Canberra: Government Printer.

COMMONWEALTH OF AUSTRALIA 1937, *The Northern Territory Investigation Committee Report*. Canberra: Government Printer.

— 1951, *Commonwealth Parliamentary Debates*, Vol. 213.

— 1952, *Commonwealth Parliamentary Debates*, Vol. 218.

COOMBS, H. C. 1972, *The future of the Australian Aboriginal*. Sydney: The University of Sydney Press.

— 1978, *Kulinma. Listening to Aboriginal Australians*. Canberra: Australian National University Press.

COURT, C. 1980, "Premier's Views on Noonkanbah". *West Australian*, 8 August.

DESPRES, L. A. 1968, "Anthropological Theory, Cultural Pluralism, and the Study of Complex Societies". *Current Anthropology*, 9(1), 3–26.

— (ed.) 1975, *Ethnicity and Resource Competition in Plural Societies*. The Hague: Mouton.

DOBBERT, M. L. 1976, "Another route to a general theory of cultural transmission: a systems model". pp. 205–212 in J. I. ROBERTS & S. K. AKINSANYA (eds), *Educational Patterns and Cultural Configurations*. New York: David McKay.

DUFTY, D. G. 1970, *Teaching about Society: Problems and Possibilities*. Sydney: Rigby.

EADES, D. 1981, " 'That's our way of talking'. Aborigines in Southeast Queeensland". *Social Alternatives*, 2(2), 11–14.

EDELMAN, M. 1971, *Politics as Symbolic Action*. Chicago: Markham.

— 1977, *Political language. Words that Succeed and Policies that Fail*. New York: Academic Press.

ELKIN, A. P. 1954, *The Australian Aborigines*. Sydney: Angus & Robertson.

— 1964, *The Australian Aborigines*. Fourth Edition. Sydney: Angus & Robertson.

ENCEL, S. 1970, "Class and Status". pp. 149–179 in A. F. DAVIES & S. ENCEL (eds), *Australian Society. A Sociological Introduction*. Second Edition. Melbourne: Cheshire.

ENGEL, F. 1978, *The Position of the Australian Aborigines*. Sydney: Australian Council of Churches.

ENLOE, C. H. 1981, "The growth of the state and ethnic mobilization: the American experience". *Ethnic and Racial Studies*, 4(2), 123–36.

EVANS, R., SAUNDERS, K., & CRONIN, K. 1975, *Exclusion, Exploitation and Extermination*. Sydney: ANZ Books.

FOLEY, M. 1981, "From protection to laissez-faire. Prospects for legislation and Social Policy affecting Queensland Aborigines and Islanders". *Social Alternatives*, 2(2), 37–41.

FORD, G. W. 1970, "Work". pp. 84–145 in A. F. DAVIES & S. ENCEL (eds), *Australian Society. A Sociological Introduction*. Second Edition. Melbourne: Cheshire.

— 1974, "Migrants, employment and employment relations in Australia". In

IMMIGRATION ADVISORY COUNCIL, *Committee on Community Relations, Interim Report*. Appendix H(i). Canberra: Australian Government Publishing Service.

FOSTER, L. E. 1981, *Australian Education. A Sociological Perspective*. Sydney: Prentice-Hall of Australia.

FOUCAULT, M. 1977, "The political function of the intellectual". *Radical Philosophy*, 17, 12–14.

FRASER, M. 1978, Migrant Services and Programs. Statement by the Prime Minister, the Rt. Hon. Malcolm Fraser. Commonwealth of Australia (mimeo).

FURNIVALL, J. S. 1948, *Colonial Policy and Practice: A Comparative Study of Burma and Netherlands India*. Cambridge: Cambridge University Press.

GALBALLY, F. 1978, *Migrant Services and Programs*. Report of the Review of Post-Arrival Programs and Services for Migrants (the Galbally Report). May 1978, Vol. 1, Volume 2 — Appendices. Canberra: Australian Government Publishing Service.

GALE, G. F., & BROOKMAN, A. 1975, *Race Relations in Australia — The Aborigines*. Sydney: McGraw-Hill.

GALLIE, W. B. 1955–6, "Essentially contested concepts". *Proceedings of the Aristotelian Society*, 56, 167–98.

GEERTZ, C. 1966, "Religion as a cultural system". pp. 1–46 in M. BANTON (ed.), *Anthropological Approaches to the Study of Religion*. London: Tavistock.

— 1973, *The interpretation of cultures; Selected essays*. New York: Basic Books.

GILBERT, K. 1977, *Living Black, Blacks talk to Kevin Gilbert*. Harmondsworth: Penguin.

GOODENOUGH, W. H. 1964, "Cultural Anthropology and Linguistics". pp. 36–39 in D. HYMES (ed.), *Language in Culture and Society*. New York: Harper & Row.

GORDON, M. M. 1964, *Assimilation in American life: the Role of Race, Religion and National Origins*. New York: Oxford University Press.

GOULD, J. 1964, "Ideology". pp. 315–317 in J. GOULD & W. L. KOLB (eds), *A Dictionary of the Social Sciences*. London: Tavistock.

GRAMSCI, A. 1971, *Selections from the Prison Notebooks of Antonio Gramsci*. Edited and translated by Q. HOARE & G. N. SMITH. London: Lawrence and Wishart.

GRASSBY, A. J. 1973a, *A Multi-cultural society for the future*. Canberra: Australian Government Publishing Service.

— 1973b, *Australia's decade of decision*. Canberra: Australian Government Publishing Service.

— 1974a, *Foreign Languages in Australia*. Immigration Reference Paper. Canberra: Australian Government Publishing Service.

— 1974b, *Australian Citizenship Policy: Our Objectives*. Canberra: Australian Government Publishing Service.

— 1974c, *Credo for a Nation*. Immigration Reference Paper. Canberra: Australian Government Publishing Service.

GREEN, A. 1982, "In defence of anti-racist teaching". *Multicultural Education*, 10(2), 19–35.

HALSEY, A. H., HEATH, A. F., & RIDGE, J. M. 1980, *Origins and Destinations. Family, Class, and Education in Modern Britain*. Oxford: Clarendon Press.

HARRIS, R. McL. 1979, "Anglo-conformism, Interactionism and Cultural Pluralism: A Study of Australian Attitudes to Migrants". pp. 23–39 in P. R. DE LACEY & M. E. POOLE (eds), *Mosaic or Melting Pot. Cultural Evolution in Australia*. Sydney: Harcourt Brace Jovanovich.

HECHTER, M. 1975, *Internal Colonialism*. Berkeley: University of California Press.

HIGHAM, J. 1975, *Send These to Me: Jews and other immigrants in Urban America*. New York: Atheneum Press.

JABUKOWICZ, A., & BUCKLEY, B. 1975, *Migrants and the Legal System*. Canberra: Australian Government Publishing Service.

JOHANSON, D. 1962, "History of the White Australia Policy". Ch. 1 in K. RIVETT (ed.), *Immigration: Control or Colour Bar*. Melbourne: Melbourne University Press.

JUPP, J. 1966, *Arrivals and Departures*. Melbourne: Cheshire-Lansdowne.

KALLEN, H. 1956, *Cultural Pluralism and the American Idea*. Philadelphia: University of Philadelphia Press.

KEESING, R. 1976, *Cultural Anthropology: a Contemporary Perspective*. New York: Holt, Rinehart & Winston.

KOLIG, E. 1977, "From tribesman to citizen? Change and continuity in social identities among south Kimberley Aborigines". In R. M. BERNDT (ed.), *Aborigines and Change: Australia in the '70s*. Canberra: Australian Institute of Aboriginal Studies.

KOVACS, M. L., & CROPLEY, A. J. 1975, *Immigrants and Society: Alienation and Assimilation*. Sydney: McGraw-Hill.

KRINGAS, P., & LEWINS, F. 1981, *Why ethnic schools? Selected case studies*. Canberra: Australian National University Press.

KROEBER, A. L., & KLUCKHOHN, C. 1952, "Culture: A Critical Review of Concepts and Definitions". *Papers of the Peabody Museum of American Archaeology and Ethnology*, 47(1).

LANGTON, M. 1981, "Urbanizing Aborigines. The Social Scientists' Great Deception". *Social Alternatives*, 2(2), 16–22.

LEACH, E. R. 1976, *Culture and Communication. The logic by which symbols are connected*. Cambridge: Cambridge University Press.

LEPERVANCHE, M. DE 1980, "From Race to Ethnicity". *Australian and New Zealand Journal of Sociology*, 16(1), 1980, 24–37.

LEWINS, F. 1980, "Ethnic schools and multiculturalism in Australia". *Journal of Intercultural Studies*, 1(2), 30–39.

LEWIS, O. 1966, *La Vida*. New York: Random House.

LIBERMAN, K. 1981, "Aboriginal Education: the School at Strelley, Western Australia". *Harvard Educational Review*, 51(1), 139–144.

LIFFMAN, M. 1979, "The Galbally Report: An Overview". *Migration Action*, IV(1), 14.

LYNCH, P. 1972, "Australia's Immigration Policy". pp. 1–12 in H. ROBERTS (ed.), *Australia's Immigration Policy*. Perth: University of Western Australia Press.

MACKELLAR, M. J. R. 1976, *Towards a Population Policy for Australia*. Address to the Stable Population (ZPG, SA) Forum, Adelaide, 9 August. Canberra: Department of Immigration and Ethnic Affairs.

— 1978, Speech by the Hon. M. J. R. MacKellar, MP, Minister for Immigration and Ethnic Affairs on Immigration Policies and Australia's Population, Ministerial Statement. ("Parliamentary Debates", 7 June 1978.) Canberra: Australian Government Publishing Service.

MACKIE, J. A. C. 1977, "Asian Migration and Australian Racial Attitudes". *Ethnic Studies*, 1(2), 1–13.

MCCONNOCHIE, K. 1981, "Background Notes on Aboriginal Education". Paper given to the joint NZARE-AARE Seminar on Multicultural Education, Massey University, Palmerston North, 2 December (mimeo).

— 1981, "Innovation and Aboriginal Education". Paper given to the joint NZARE-AARE Seminar, Massey University, Palmerston North, 2 December (mimeo).

MCEWEN, Hon. J. 1939, *Commonwealth Government Policy with Respect to Aboriginals*. White Paper. Canberra: Ministry for the Interior.

MCLAREN, J. 1968, *Our Troubled Schools*. Melbourne: Cheshire.

MCMAHON, W., Rt. Hon. 1972, Statement by the Prime Minister the Rt. Hon. William McMahon. Australian Aborigines; Commonwealth Policy and Achievements. In GALE & BROOKMAN, op. cit., 84–86.

MADDOCK, K. 1974, *The Australian Aborigines. A Portrait of their Society*. Harmondsworth: Penguin.

MARTIN, J. I. 1972, *Migrants: Equality and Ideology*. Meredith Memorial Lectures, 1972. Bundoora: La Trobe University.

— 1976a, "Ethnic Pluralism and Identity". In S. MURRAY-SMITH (ed.), *Melbourne Studies in Education 1976*. Melbourne: Melbourne University Press.

— 1976b, "The Education of Migrant Children in Australia". pp. 1–65 in C. A. PRICE & J. I. MARTIN (eds), *Australian Immigration. A bibliography and digest*. Number 3, 1975, Part 2. Canberra: The Australian National University, Department of Demography.

— 1976c, "Education in a Multicultural Society". Paper presented to the Conference on Education in a Multicultural Society, New South Wales Teachers' Federation, Sydney, 26–27 November (mimeo).

— 1978, *The Migrant Presence*. Sydney: George Allen & Unwin.

MARTIN, J. J., & COX, D. 1975, *Welfare of Migrants*. Canberra: Australian Government Publishing Service.

MARTINDALE, D. 1961, *The Nature and Types of Sociological Theory*. London: Routledge & Kegan Paul.

MARX, K. 1870, *A Contribution to the Critique of Political Economy*. Moscow: Progress Publishers.

MILLER, S. M. 1967, *Breaking the Credentials Barrier*. New York: Ford Foundation.

MURPHY, R. 1971, *The Dialectics of Social Life*. London: Allen & Unwin.

MUSGRAVE, P. W. 1965, *The Sociology of Education*. London: Methuen.

NATIONAL SEMINAR FOR TEACHER EDUCATORS 1974, *The Multi-Cultural Society*. Seminar Proceedings, Macquarie University, 28–31 August 1974. Canberra: Australian Department of Education in co-operation with the Australian Department of Labor and Immigration.

OSBORNE, G. 1978, "A Socialist Dilemma". 112–128 in A. CURTHOYS & A. MARKUS (eds), *Who are our enemies?* Sydney: Hale and Iremonger.

PARKIN, F. (ed.) 1974, *The Social Analysis of Class Structure*. London: Tavistock.

PRATTE, R. 1979, *Pluralism in Education*. Springfield, Ill.: Charles C. Thomas.

PRICE, C. A. 1974, *The Great White Walls are Built*. Canberra: Australian National University Press.

REDFIELD, M. P. (ed.) 1962, *Human Nature and the study of Society*. The Papers of Robert Redfield, Volume 1. Chicago: University of Chicago Press.

ROOTH, J. S. 1968, "The immigration programme". pp. 57–62 in H. THROSSWELL (ed.), *Ethnic Minorities in Australia. The Welfare of Aborigines and Migrants*. Sydney: Australian Council of Social Services.

ROWLEY, C. D. 1970, *The Destruction of Aboriginal Society*. Canberra: Australian National University Press.

— 1972, *Outcasts in White Australia*. Harmondsworth: Penguin.

SCHERMERHORN, R. A. 1970, *Comparative Ethnic Relations. A Framework for Theory and Research*. New York: Random House.

SCHNEIDER, L., & BONJEAN, C. (eds) 1973, *The Idea of Culture in the Social Services*. Cambridge: Cambridge University Press.

SCHOOLS COMMISSION INTERIM COMMITTEE 1973, *Schools in Australia: Report of the Interim Committee for the Australian Schools Commission* (The Karmel Report). Canberra: Australian Government Publishing Service.

SCHOOLS COMMISSION 1975, *Report for the Triennium 1976–78*. Canberra: Australian Government Publishing Service.

— 1981, *Report for the Triennium 1982–84*. Canberra: Australian Government Publishing Service.

SMITH, L. R. 1980, *The Aboriginal Population of Australia*. Canberra.

SMITH, M. G. 1965, *The plural society in the British West Indies*. Berkeley: University of California Press.

— 1982, "Ethnicity and ethnic groups in America: the view from Harvard". *Ethnic and Racial Studies*, 5(1), 1–22.

SMOLICZ, J. J. 1971, "Is the Australian school an assimilationist agency?" *Education News*, 13(4), 4–8.

— 1981, "Cultural Pluralism and Educational Policy: In Search of Stable Multiculturalism". *The Australian Journal of Education*, 25(2), 121–145.

SNEDDEN, W. 1969, *The Age*, 19 September.

SOUTER, G. 1972, "The invasion of Arnhem Land". *Sydney Morning Herald*. 22 July, 20.

STANNER, W. E. H. 1969, *After the Dreaming. The Boyer Lectures 1968*. Sydney: Australian Broadcasting Commission.

— 1979, *White Man Got No Dreaming*. Canberra: Australian National University Press.

STEVENS, F. 1969, "Weipa: the Politics of Pauperization". *Australian Quarterly*, 41(3), 5–25.

— 1970, "Aborigines". pp. 362–412 in A. F. DAVIES & S. ENCEL (eds), *Australian Society. An Introduction*. Second Edition. Melbourne: Cheshire.

STOCKLEY, D. 1978, "The Fraser Governments, Migrants and Education". Paper presented at the Australian Political Studies Association Annual Conference. 30 August – 1 September. Adelaide (mimeo).

STORER, D. (ed.) 1975, *Ethnic Rights Power and Participation*. Melbourne: Clearing House on Migration Issues, Ecumenical Migration Centre, and Centre for Urban Research and Action.

SUTTON, P. 1981, "Land rights and compensation in settled Australia". *Social Alternatives*, 2(2), 6–10.

THERNSTROM, S., ORLOV, A., & HANDLIN, O. (eds) 1980, *Harvard Encyclopaedia of American Ethnic Groups*. Cambridge, Mass.: Harvard University Press.

THOMPSON, L. 1969, *The Secret of Culture. Nine Community Studies*. New York: Random House.

TUMIN, M. M. 1977, "Introduction". pp. xii–xx in M. M. TUMIN & W. PLOTCH (eds), *Pluralism in a Democratic Society*. New York: Praeger.

TURNBULL, C. 1956, *Black War*. Melbourne: Cheshire.

TYLOR, E. B. 1871, *Primitive Culture*. London: John Murray.

VALENTINE, C. 1969, *Culture and Poverty*. Chicago: University of Chicago Press.

VAN DEN BERGHE, P. L. 1975, "Ethnicity and class in Highland Peru". In L. DESPRES (ed.), *Ethnicity and Resource Competition in Plural Societies*. The Hague: Mouton.

WAGLEY, C., & HARRIS, M. 1958, *Minorities in the New World*. New York: Columbia University Press.

WARNECKE, R. 1981, "Do we really want a multi-culture?" *The Age*, 2 October.

WATTS, B. H. 1981, *Aboriginal Futures: Review of Research and Developments and Related Policies in the Education of Aborigines*, Vol. 1. Brisbane: Schonell Education Research Centre.

WEBER, M. 1968, *Economy and Society*. Edited by G. ROTH & C. WITTICH. New York: Bedminster Press.

WENTWORTH, W. C. 1971, *The Australian*, 9 May, 4.

WILLIAMS, R. 1973, "Base and Superstructure in Marxist Cultural Theory". *New Left Review*, LXXXII (November/December).

WILLIAMS, R. 1977, *Marxism and Literature*. Oxford: Oxford University Press.

WISEMAN, R. 1974, "Some issues involved in ethnic pluralism and education in Australia". *The Forum of Education*, 33(2), September, 146–163.

YARWOOD, A. T., & KNOWLING, M. J. 1982, *Race Relations in Australia. A History*. Sydney: Methuen.

YOUNG, M. F. D. (ed.) 1971, *Knowledge and Control: New Directions for the Sociology of Education*. London: Collier-Macmillan.

YOUNG, R. 1977, "Multicultural education in New South Wales". Paper presented to the Education Section of the ANZAAS Congress, August 1977 (mimeo).

ZUBRZYCKI, J. 1977, "The Formation of the Australian Ethnic Affairs Council". Speech to the Inaugural Meeting by the Chairman, Professor Jerzy Zubrzycki, MBE, FASSA, Canberra, 23 March 1977. *Ethnic Studies*, 1(2), 62–67.

— 1979, "Limits to multiculturalism". Paper given at a Centre for Migrant Studies Seminar, Melbourne, Monash University, 17 September, 1979 (mimeo).

Index